I Want to Enjoy My Children

Let your father and mother be glad and let her who bore you rejoice.

Proverbs 23:25

Biblical Principles for Parenting

Dr. Henry Brandt • Kerry L. Skinner

0-9648743-0-X

Dewey Decimal Classification: 261.8

Subject Heading: Parent and child

Library of Congress Cataloging-in-Publication Data

Brandt, Henry and Skinner, Kerry L.

I want to enjoy my children Workbook / by Henry Brandt and Kerry L.
Skinner.

p.   cm.

ISBN 0-9648743-0-X

CONTENTS

PREFACE

Here is a wonderful word picture of a human being.

> Oh, the comfort, the inexpressible comfort, of feeling safe with a person. Having neither to weigh thoughts nor measure words, but pouring all right out just as they are, chaff and grain together, certain that a faithful friendly hand will take and sift them, keep what is worth keeping, and with a breath of understanding, blow the rest away.
>
> George Eliot

What would a man give for a wife like that? Probably as much as a woman would give for such a husband.

At age 44, Homer Dowdy and I wrote *Building a Christian Home*. We said the trail was downhill when the family reaches the "empty nest" stage. We were wrong. The trail got steeper. In fact, the steepest part came after we reached age 60.

At age 76 the view from this elevation is magnificent. It was hard work getting here. The trail ahead is still steep. Now I can look back down the trail all the way to the bottom. There are people just beginning the climb. Some have started up the trail. If only they could see what I see, it would make a difference how they prepare for the climb.

A brief review of that book written thirty years ago bears repeating here.

Reviewing the elements of family living brings to mind a personal experience in mountain climbing. With three companions we stood at the top of a glacier, astounded at the breathtaking view eight thousand feet below. There was a solemn quietness at the top. What a thrill, what joy, what a sense of accomplishment in achieving the summit. We stood speechless, drinking in the vastness of the wide world at our feet.

It had been an eight-hour climb over unfamiliar, rugged terrain. Poorly-fitting shoes had caused several blisters. A fall, ending on a rock, netted a painful bruise. One hand throbbed with pain because it had grabbed hold of a thorny branch. At one point we came to a sheer cliff. A more experienced member of the party started up. We watched, uncertainly. Loose boulders came hurtling past us and bounced on to the base of the mountain, but our friend made it and we were encouraged to climb.

Once there was a steep snow field to cross. Slipping and sliding made our hearts race wildly and it took courage even to move. Then came long, shady trails, covered with soft, cool moss and lined with great timbers. Swift, clear streams and lacy waterfalls were close by.

At last, we reached the summit—tired, aching, hungry, but victorious and satisfied. It was worth the effort. We were happy.

Many persons have looked up at those gleaming, snow-capped peaks and that glacier, which seemed so near, so accessible, so inviting. Some have started out to conquer them, filled with enthusiasm and purpose, yet the climb upward has filled them with fear. The miles have proved disappointing and disheartening. The distance is greater than anticipated and the ascent much steeper. They have become utterly unappreciative of the quiet valleys, the great trees, the roaring rapids and mighty waterfalls. Instead, they have become increasingly aware of tired muscles, sore feet, exhaustion, and dampness. Somewhere along the way, facing a particularly difficult grade, courage has faltered and purpose has died. It is time to reconsider the goal. Sadly, they have given up. They have turned around and headed home. They were unprepared or unwilling to face the obstacles.

The successful ones, starting out on the same journey, have found pleasure and challenge in the very roughness and hardness of the journey. They have found joy in the same difficulties that overwhelmed the others. The struggle up the mountain has become rewarding, though exhausting. Success in mastering a slope inspired courage and hope for tackling the next one.

Mountain climbing consists of beautiful vistas, long periods of uninteresting, undesirable stretches, bracing air, steep and difficult places, danger, strain, pain, and cooperation. Mountain climbers depend on each other, sustain, pull up, and boost each other. The demands and dependence on one another build a bond of friendship among the climbers—or they can cause rifts and conflicts to develop.

This summit view affords an appraising look at marriage. All who marry start out hand in hand with their hopes high, joyously, with lively, eager anticipation. As they look up the trail, a life together, establishing a home, raising a family, all beckon. It all seems so easy to attain, so inviting.

Marriage is not like walking along a familiar trail that you have explored many times and for which you know every twist and turn along the way. Marriage, rather, is more like a strange trail with every turn holding something new. There are pleasant stretches easily mastered. Then, there are steep, rugged places which leave you aching and exhausted. One fact in life is certain: "the certainty of uncertainty." The mature Christian makes his way along the trail with keen interest, enjoying the variety, the unexpected and getting satisfaction out of meeting the challenges of a new baby in the family, a promotion, a move into another house, sickness, death, accidents, or a new life.

Each change, with the problems that it brings, exposes the soul. In decision making, your values and goals come into play. We have the promise:

The humble He guides in justice, And the humble He teaches His way.
PSALM 25:9

Such a man can gather the facts, sift them and come to a decision that will be according to God's way.

There are many natural changes that come to a married couple. You pass from the family founding stage to the childbearing, childrearing, childlaunching, and the empty nest.

There are unexpected surprises at each stage. Soon after being married, Ken discovered that Pat snored. They were at odds over the tempo their life together should take. They had arrived at the first steep climb in their marriage and the summit did not seem so easy to reach. Both however, were sincere Christians and they turned to God for wisdom and strength to solve these problems. They found a solution and through it learned of the help that God can give a couple including the renewed hope and courage needed to face the next challenge.

Not so with Wally and Marge. He insists that she is not neat enough around the house. She says her appearance behind closed doors is her own business. Wally wants Marge to care for the flowers and shrubs, but complains that she spends too much money in doing so. Her reply? Do it yourself, mister! Before the first real rise in the trail is reached, their progress forward has slackened and they have begun to complain.

Preparation for marriage consists of two important commitments: First, to love God with all your heart, soul and mind, and, second, to love your neighbor as yourself. God would have you love everyone with a love that has at least nine components: patience, kindness, generosity, humility, courtesy, unselfishness, good temper, purity of heart, and sincerity.

Two persons who set out to love each other in this way—which Drummond calls the "spectrum of love"—sooner or later discover themselves incapable of loving another person in this way. They discover they cannot live up to such virtues before God.

But fortunate are those who have acknowledged that they are weak and inadequate and who have discovered that in Jesus Christ lies the strength and courage necessary for their journey. As Paul the apostle put it,

Therefore we do not lose heart. Even though our outward man is perishing, yet the inward man is being renewed day by day. For our light affliction, which is but for a moment, is working for us a far more exceeding and eternal weight of glory, while we do not look at the things which are seen, but at the things which are not seen. For the things which are seen are temporary, but the things which are not seen are eternal.
2 CORINTHIANS 4:16-18

It is the spiritual man who is renewed day by day. The spiritual man is renewed in comfort and consolation (2 Corinthians 1:3-5), in patience and joy (Colossians

1:11), wisdom (James 1:5), righteousness (Philippians 3:9) and in peace and hope (Romans 15:13).

The serious Christian couple, recognizing their need of Christ as Savior and source of renewed life, will not be overwhelmed by the stresses and strains of the journey. Their mutual objective is to please God and to serve Him. As they master one obstacle after another, through the grace of Christ, they can say with increasing certainty what Isaiah said,

"For the Lord God will help Me; Therefore I will not be disgraced; Therefore I have set My face like flint, And I know that I will not be ashamed."
Isaiah 50:7

The journey along the marital trail requires careful balance, lest you tumble headlong into disaster. Men must balance their roles as husband, father, employer or employee, son, and churchman, among others. For the women, there are the roles of wife, mother, daughter, churchwoman, and employer or employee. For both, there is the vital role of being a person. The world is a fascinating place and offers many interesting things to do. But to keep your life in a proper healthy balance, careful study and often sacrifice are required.

A wholesome marriage also requires good will, cooperation, and dedication. It implies two free people who voluntarily make their way on the same trail with the husband taking the lead. The spirit permeating a wholesome marriage is beautifully described by Paul,

Now I plead with you, brethren, by the name of our Lord Jesus Christ, that you all speak the same thing, and that there be no divisions among you, but that you be perfectly joined together in the same mind and in the same judgment.
1 Corinthians 1:10

Those who must have their own way find these requirements too steep, their steps falter and they consider turning back.

An endless shelf of books has been written to describe these stages. In our day, we need not be taken by surprise by the nature of parenthood. For each of these stages Havighurst aptly describes the growth process as a series of "developmental tasks." He defines a developmental task as one which "arises at or about a certain period in the life of an individual, successful achievement of which leads to his happiness and to success with later tasks, while failure leads to unhappiness in the individual, disapproval by the society and difficulty with later tasks."

Familiarity with these stages can be acquired. It involves purpose, vision, effort. The resources are available and can be mastered by the mature person. Guiding a child, then, through the various stages involves knowledge, maturity, certainty. The task is described in Proverbs 22:6,

**Train up a child in the way he should go, And
when he is old he will not depart from it.**

Training, or discipline, includes everything you do in order to help the child learn. It involves the home, school, church, and other agencies. It is a twenty-year process. The major task is to teach your children from the beginning that you are followers of the Master, that they need Christ as Savior, that they should keep God central in their lives, and that you look for the return of Christ.

Guiding children involves a purpose and a goal. Parents must assume responsibility for influencing children and making their learning right ways effective. As you study the job you will find you have made mistakes. But dedicated, purposeful loving effort will enable you to correct those mistakes. Failure to understand the stages of a child's growth as well your own will cause progress along the trail to be most difficult.

As your children grow, you have the important task of teaching them a sense of reverence and awe toward their own bodies. Their God-given power to pass life on to someone else must also be learned. You will do this in simple ways. Your attitude about the body will be taught as you cuddle the child, bathe him, go through the toilet-training process, and give him answers to his questions. The relationship between you and your partner will contribute greatly to his concept of how a man and woman should treat each other.

As the child becomes aware of the opposite sex, he should understand the normality of this attraction, the value of careful management of it, and the importance of physical contact being an expression of the deepest love, loyalty and devotion. A mature, genuine, wholesome person, rightly related to others and to God is ready to choose a mate and go on to found his own family.

When the last child has been launched, you and your partner will face a new challenge. This great day should bring a sense of accomplishment. If you have given your best to the job, you will enter the empty-nest stage with the satisfaction of a job well done.

We may liken the beginning of the empty-nest stage to arriving at the summit after a long climb up the mountain. This is the top. What joy to be here. True, all trails lead downward, but the couple at the summit soon realize that the trail down tugs on a set of muscles other than those used on the way up. It takes energy and effort to get down from the top. And as on the upward trail, there are pleasant places and danger spots on the way down.

When a couple's nest becomes empty, they still have important tasks to look forward to. Success in this stage will depend on your preparation. Your approach to past stages will no doubt be a good indication of how you will approach this one. The basic requirements are the same—love, unity, and dedication to God. The specific tasks involved include resuming your life as a couple, developing a new relationship with your children (and learning how to get on with your grandchildren), use of more leisure time, decreasing physical strength, retirement, and perhaps reduced income.

Preparation will involve study, careful planning, and effort.

Sooner or later the day will come that all travelers look forward to with keen anticipation and joy—the time when the end of the trail is reached. It will not be so important that the journey was less difficult and trying than others you have experienced. Of prime importance will be the fact of getting there, that you have held true to the course, and that you have achieved your clearly defined objectives.

Let us go to Paul one last time,

And be found in Him, not having my own righteousness, which is from the law, but that which is through faith in Christ, the righteousness which is from God by faith; that I may know Him and the power of His resurrection, and the fellowship of His sufferings, being conformed to His death, if, by any means, I may attain to the resurrection from the dead.
PHILIPPIANS 3:9-11

The one who can look back on a lifetime of preparation for this day can anticipate the same reception that the servant received when his lord returned after a long absence,

Well done, good and faithful servant; you were faithful over a few things; I will make you ruler over many things. Enter into the joy of your Lord.
MATTHEW 25:21

OBSERVATIONS

We wrote that some of the steep places along the trail will be the birth of a child, a job change, moving, accidents, sickness, death, and new responsibilities. We have experienced all of them and more. We hadn't expected all of them to happen to us. We have observed that to handle the climb lovingly is indeed a human impossibility. You need a Savior and access to the Spirit of God. Both are there for the asking.

We did not foresee the role of the woman changing so swiftly from full-time homemaker to full-time in the work force. We did not foresee that the guidance and training of children would be done by people outside the family circle. We did not foresee the divorce rate, increase in violence and cruelty, and the collapse of Biblical values.

We discovered that the "empty nest" mark is not the summit. When we got there we were surprised. There were several gleaming snow-covered peaks ahead. The climb from the 56 mark to the 76 mark was the most painful, difficult, and demanding climb of them all. Ahead of us it looks like another steep climb, and beyond that peak is eternity.

We can look down the trail. There is some congestion at about the age fifty or sixty mark. The people on the trail have the latest climbing clothes and equipment. They appear to be well-fed. Below them are some bedazzling brilliantly lit places. Instead of continuing up the trail we see the backs of many well-equipped climbers. The trail up is too narrow, stressful, and steep. The trail to those brilliantly lit places is down hill and much more comfortable. From here those places look like idols. They look like houses, cars, luxury hotels, fabulous restaurants, theaters, the latest hospitals, and things like that. They are going downhill to a life of ease. After all, didn't they spend a lifetime to gain these idols?

They will never see the trail from my vista. If they could they would keep climbing.

For what is a man profited if he gains the whole world, and loses his own soul?
MATTHEW 16:26

If there is a single major point to make, we would put this one on in bright lights—It is the spiritual man who is renewed day by day. Renewed in:
•Comfort and consolation—2 Corinthians 1:3-5
•Patience and joy—Colossians 1:11
•Wisdom—James 1:5
•Righteousness—Philippians 3:9
•Peace and Hope—Romans 15:13

The serious Christian couple, recognizing their need of Christ as Savior and source of renewed life, will not be overwhelmed by the stresses and strains of the journey.

CENTRALITY OF THE BIBLE

How seriously do you take the Bible? Does it really make any difference to you what it says? If you read something about parent-child relations in the Bible which contradicts what you read in another book, would you reject what the Bible says, or would you reject what the other book says?

For me, the Bible is not on trial; the other book is. The speaker is on trial, not the Bible. If he contradicts what the scriptures say, I'll stay with the scriptures.

I am writing about family living from my lofty perch at age 76. Our oldest child has had his 50th birthday. When Eva and I learned that she was carrying her first child I was age 26. You might say we were at the foot of a magnificent mountain. We were eager to start the climb. It turned out to be steeper and more demanding than we expected.

UNIT 1

GROWING WITH YOUR CHILDREN

THOUGHT STARTER
Parental growth is as important as the physical, mental, emotional,
and spiritual growth of your children.

MEMORY VERSE
**Train up a child in the way he should go, And when
he is old he will not depart from it.**
PROVERBS 22:6

DAY 1—FAMILY DEVELOPMENT

Launching and completing a marriage and a family can be compared to
launching and completing a college education.

John, a high-school senior, is a brilliant student, mostly A's; a fine athlete; a
four-letter man; popular socially; president of his class and well-liked; from a happy
Christian home; busy at his church, and active in his youth group. We can
confidently say that John has a fine background for success in college.

Even so, when he goes to college, John at best will be an outstanding freshman.
We would not expect him to possess the knowledge, the experience, the maturity, the
judgment, or the social graces of the college senior. Such qualities are the result of
four years of class attendance, study, practice, contact with others, effort, persistence,
and choices that contribute to his development. Becoming a successful, well-adjusted
college senior is a four-year process, even for the most talented freshman.

In the women's section of a local newspaper, there appeared a write-up on the
wedding of two popular young people. Janet and Jim, the
couple, have started out on their marriage. Each brings a
particular background to it. Although outstanding in
qualifications, they are at best just beginners at the task of
marriage. We do not expect them to possess the wisdom of
seasoned veterans who have raised a fine family and who
now look on as their children establish their own homes.

> *"Although
> outstanding in
> qualifications, they
> are at best just
> beginners at the task
> of marriage."*

Both of them are college graduates. Academically,
both of them were in the top ten of their classes. They were both leaders in college

1

activities. She has a position in a prestigious law firm. She is being trained as a legal secretary. He has an enviable position with an international accounting firm. He has been chosen to begin a four-year training program to prepare for a leadership position. They have now been married four years. Their careers, their marriage, and a pleasant social life keep them fully occupied.

An unexpected event has come into their lives. Janet is nine months pregnant. Miracle of miracles, she will soon have a baby. At best, that baby will receive a reluctant welcome. Its parents must shift their way of life. They would prefer to live like they are now—without the parenting responsibility.

Do you know of couples in this position? Why do you think many couples prefer a career to parenting?

_____

_____

_____

Reluctant, Inexperienced Parents

The creator of the world has obviously chosen to give the responsibility for guiding the life of a baby to young, inexperienced people. They hardly know what marriage is all about. They are just getting started with their careers. They look forward to exploring a fascinating world. Now they are tied down to a baby. They hardly know where to start. They will hopefully, even if reluctantly, accept the task.

There is help available. Janet and Jim are good, capable students. Will they choose to grow along with their baby? Their parents had to make that choice, and now it's their turn. The future of that baby is in their hands.

> *"The creator of the world has obviously chosen to give the responsibility for guiding the life of a baby to young, inexperienced people."*

Stages in Family Development

Parenting, like a college education, is a process. It requires years of study, effort, persistence, and choices that contribute to the wholesome development of the marriage.

The following chart shows some of the stages that a typical marriage passes through. It is difficult to describe any one marriage. Each of the stages may be longer or shorter than the average. Some families are in several stages at one time. Some marriages are interrupted by divorce or death. The chart does show clearly that most marriages pass through a series of stages that are well-defined and can be anticipated and prepared for.

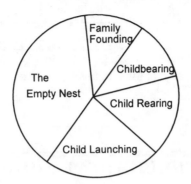

I will use my marital stages as an example:

Family founding	2 years	Age 24-26
Child bearing	4 years	Age 26-30
Child rearing	22 years	Age 26-48, last child out of high school
Child launching	10 years	Age 44-54, last child out of college
Empty nest	29 years	Age 48-78,

Note: child-bearing, rearing, launching and empty-nest stages overlap.

Take a moment to chart your stages even if you have just begun.

_____

_____

_____

_____

A study of the chart shows that my family had a very brief period, two years, before the childbearing stage began. In other words, marriage usually implies parenthood.

APPLICATION (OBEDIENCE TO GOD)

What did God teach me today:

_____

_____

Applying what God is pointing out to you is essential. How will you obey the Lord today?

_____

_____

Write a short prayer to God that summarizes your thoughts.

_____

_____

What are you going to do, say, or think today that will demonstrate obedience to God?

_____

_____

THOUGHT FOR THE DAY
Parenthood implies the responsibility for
training the children.

DAY 2—THE DEVELOPMENTAL TASK

One of the most useful helps to the parent is the concept of the "developmental task." Simply stated it refers to certain tasks that arise in a person's life at various age levels. His happiness or success with later tasks depends on his ability to perform these tasks successfully. Havighurst[1] describes the tasks a person must learn—the developmental tasks of life—as:

> those things which constitute healthy and satisfactory growth in our society. They are the things a person must learn if he is to be judged and to judge himself to be a reasonably happy and successful person. A developmental task is a task which arises at or about a certain period in the life of an individual, successful achievement of which leads to his happiness and to success with later tasks, while failure leads to unhappiness in the individual, disapproval by the society and difficulty with later tasks.

Considering the task of learning to talk, Havighurst explains,

> Sometime between the ages of one and two most children master the essentials of human speech and language…If the task is not learned, the failure will stand in the way of learning a series of later tasks, which depend greatly upon language.

4

There are two reasons why this concept is helpful to educators, Havighurst says. Since parents are educators, too, we will transfer his reasoning from the school to the home. First of all learning helps the parents to discover the nature of the job confronting them. Second, it helps give some idea of the timing of their efforts. It assists them in discovering when conditions are most favorable for learning these tasks, a time which Havighurst calls "the teachable moment." Here is how he describes it.

> *"Learning helps the parents to discover the nature of the job confronting them."*

The Teachable Moment

When the body is ripe, and society requires, and the self is ready to achieve a certain task, the teachable moment has come.

For that reason we include here a series of developmental tasks that are normal for the indicated age levels. These are adapted from Havighurst. To receive maximum benefit from this list, refer to the section that applies to your child and notice what tasks he is presently facing. To know these will help you train your child to meet these responsibilities and keep you from expecting too much.

Infancy And Early Childhood
1. Learning God loves them by learning a sense of trust.
2. Learning to walk.
3. Learning to eat solid foods.
4. Learning to talk.
5. Learning to control the elimination of body wastes.
6. Learning sex differences and sexual modesty.
7. Achieving physiological stability.
8. Forming simple concepts of social and physical reality.
9. Learning to relate one's self emotionally to parents, siblings and other people.
10. Learning to distinguish right from wrong and developing a conscience.

Middle Childhood (age 6 to 12)
1. Learning God loves them and sent Jesus for them.
2. Learning physical skills necessary for ordinary games.
3. Building wholesome attitudes toward one's self as a growing organism.
4. Learning to get along with others of own age.
5. Learning to behave like boys and girls.
6. Developing fundamental skills in reading, writing, and calculating.
7. Developing concepts necessary for everyday living.
8. Developing the conscience, morality, and a scale of values.

Adolescence (age 12 to 18)
1. Learning what obedience to God means.

2. Accepting one's body and a masculine or feminine role.

3. Developing new relationships with others of same age of both sexes.

4. Becoming emotionally independent of parents and other adults.

5. Achieving assurance of economic independence.

6. Selecting and preparing for an occupation.

7. Developing concepts and intellectual skills necessary for civic and social duty.

8. Desiring and achieving socially responsible behavior.

9. Preparing for marriage and family life.

Early Adulthood (age 18 to 30)

1. Seeking God's direction for all of the following:

2. Selecting a mate.

3. Learning to live with a marriage partner.

4. Starting a family.

5. Rearing children.

6. Managing a home.

7. Getting started in an occupation.

8. Taking on civic responsibility

9. Finding a congenial social group.

Middle Age (age 30 to 55)

1. Teaching your family to know God.

2. Achieving adult civic and social responsibility.

3. Establishing and maintaining an economic standard of living.

4. Assisting teenage children to become responsible and happy adults.

5. Deepening one's love for God with all one's heart, soul, and mind.

6. Developing adult leisure activities.

7. Falling back on the couple's role after the nest is empty.

8. Accepting and adjusting to physiological changes of middle age.

9. Adjusting to aging parents.

Later Maturity

1. Teaching grandchildren to love God.

2. Adjusting to decreasing physical strength and health.

3. Adjusting to retirement and reduced income.

4. Adjusting to death of spouse.

5. Becoming an active member of one's own age group.

6. Establishing satisfactory living arrangements.

We have included the stages of marriage and a list of adult developmental tasks because the child is not the only one who is growing; you are growing along with him. You, too, are facing developmental tasks.

Parenthood and discipline require that mothers and fathers understand the tasks, study each child, and guide the development program of each child step by step.

> *"Parenthood and discipline require that mothers and fathers understand the tasks, study each child, and guide the development program of each child step by step."*

Take a few minutes to go back through the stages of development. Place a check mark beside each stage your child has gone through or is currently in. Then, repeat the process placing a star beside the stages you have gone through or are in currently. How does this make you feel?

_____

_____

_____

_____

APPLICATION (OBEDIENCE TO GOD)

What did God teach me today:

_____

_____

Applying what God is pointing out to you is essential. How will you obey the Lord today?

_____

_____

Write a short prayer to God that summarizes your thoughts.

_____

_____

What are you going to do, say, or think today that will demonstrate obedience to God?

_____

_____

THOUGHT FOR THE DAY
Parenthood involves as much learning and growing
personally as it does for your child.

DAY 3—ME, AN EXPERT?

Growing with the first child can be likened to the school teacher who is presenting a particular course for the first time. Most likely, he can keep just one step ahead of his class and when he prepares his material he does not know whether it will be effective until he tries it out. Teaching that same course the second year is much easier—and better for the new class. He knows his material more intimately, has added to it from new sources. Since he is more confident, he spends less time in preparing. He also has other courses to teach, possibly a new one requiring development of a new set of notes and teaching outline. Thus, the job always gets bigger and more complicated.

What do you believe will make or does make your job as a parent complicated?

_____

_____

_____

_____

It is the same with the parent. You can expect to be better informed and better prepared to guide each child as he comes along. Dealing with the second child will be more "routine" than it was with the first. Things that bothered you with the first will be "old stuff" with those that come after. There will be the complication of being a parent to children of different age levels, each presenting a "teachable moment," often simultaneously, on widely differing developmental tasks.

Do you think the stages of development can be predicted? Why?

_____

_____

_____

> *"Do not make the mistake of thinking that the stages of development are steady and that progress is of a constantly accelerating speed."*

Do not make the mistake of thinking that the stages of development are steady and that progress is of a constantly accelerating speed. If you keep this in mind, you will not become discouraged when you think your child is making no headway in a given task. Rather, you will learn patience and will know that what seems to be a marking of time will someday give way to a learning of double-time cadence.

The writer of Ecclesiastes puts it this way:

To every thing there is a season, a time for every purpose under the heaven:
A time to be born, and a time to die; a time to plant,
and a time to pluck what is planted.
ECCLESIASTES 3:1, 2

Isaiah asks a question of importance to parents and then answers it:

"Whom will he teach knowledge? And whom will he make to understand the message? Those just weaned from the milk? Those just drawn from the breasts? For precept must be upon precept, precept upon precept, Line upon line, line upon line, Here a little, there a little.
ISAIAH 28:9, 10

> *"The parent must develop skill in identifying the teachable moment, that fleeting period of time when the child is ready to learn a task that must be taught."*

The parent must develop skill in identifying the teachable moment, that fleeting period of time when the child is ready to learn a task that must be taught.

As in any profession, growth, effort, and parental study never end. Changing circumstances continuously offer new challenges. As in any profession also, the best qualified parent seeks help through constant reading, organized classes, government and private agencies, and the church. By putting your ideas into practice, you will gradually acquire more and more skill in the art of arranging experiences that foster wholesome, happy development. You will thereby develop understanding and, in time, conviction.

Children who live in an atmosphere of loving effort can survive many technical mistakes. The Bible states:

> *"Children who live in an atmosphere of loving effort can survive many technical mistakes."*

**And above all things have fervent love for one another, for
"love will cover a multitude of sins."**
1 PETER 4:8

Parenthood and discipline are matters of feelings, enjoyment, spirit, and dedication, more than techniques.

Remember, you are the world's greatest expert on your children. Teachers, friends, pastors, and neighbors come and go. Only God knows your child as well as you do. Nevertheless, you need to major in the study of how to train him. Focus on knowing the development tasks he is facing, and aim to apply this knowledge in leading him in the way he ought to go.

APPLICATION (OBEDIENCE TO GOD)

What did God teach me today:

_____

_____

Applying what God is pointing out to you is essential. How will you obey the Lord today?

_____

_____

Write a short prayer to God that summarizes your thoughts.

_____

_____

What are you going to do, say, or think today that will demonstrate obedience to God?

_____

_____

THOUGHT FOR THE DAY
**Strive to become the world's greatest
expert on your children.**

D A Y 4 —TRAINING A BABY TO BECOME A MATURE ADULT

If you have read this far, you will understand when we say that successful parents must be:

1. At peace within themselves.
2. Happy, congenial partners.

Take a moment to examine your life. Are you at peace with yourself? If not, take time right now to ask God to search your heart. Are you happy with your spouse? If not, what does God need to do to adjust your life?

_____

_____

_____

_____

_____

Beginning parents have a responsibility that can be summed up in a brief Bible verse:

Train up a child in the way he should go...
PROVERBS 22:6

According to the dictionary, training and correction that produces proper conduct or action is called discipline.

Write your definition of discipline.

_____

_____

_____

_____

_____

_____

We think of a disciplined person as one who has chosen a certain way of life and voluntarily continues in his chosen way. To "discipline" a child is to teach that child the way he ought to go. This includes everything that you do in order to help children learn. Parents do their part along with the school, church, other agencies, and society in general. Discipline involves a twenty-year process. During this time you slowly relinquish complete control in favor of the gradually developing inner strengths that enable the child to take responsibility for his own conduct and its consequences.

Discipline involves teaching the child to accept activities that are not open to debate, like necessary routines at home, in school, church, and community. It involves teaching standards by which the child can judge his own behavior. It also involves teaching him to face the problems of life with confidence, hope, eagerness, and determination. The disciplined person adds daily to his fund of knowledge. His relationships bring more satisfaction than annoyance, and his attitude toward life is one of courage. He has a zest for living. If your child grows up to take upon himself this kind of life, your training of him has been good.

Parenthood launches the couple on an irreversible way of life. As children grow, they make relentless demands on the energy and ingenuity of their parents. However, children grow up in a reasonably systematic way, enabling the parent to become familiar with what to expect. A study of the developmental tasks of family living will help the parent to anticipate stages so he may help his children achieve healthy growth.

> *"Parenthood launches the couple on an irreversible way of life."*

> *"The major task is to teach the child to love God and keep His commandments."*

Discipline is everything that you do in order to train your child in the way that he should go. The major task is to teach the child to love God and keep His commandments. The tools for training are a knowledge of God's Word, a knowledge of the needs of children, a knowledge of the particular child, definite limits, and willingness to help the child with your personal supervision.

You must use all the skill, knowledge and help available to interpret and to teach your values to your children. If you can do this and enjoy the process through each swiftly passing phase, then the "discipline problem" will become a pleasant task. It is not something to make you cringe. The task of leading your children to an abundant life should be your focus.

APPLICATION (OBEDIENCE TO GOD)

What did God teach me today:

_____

_____

Applying what God is pointing out to you is essential. How will you obey the Lord today?

_____

_____

Write a short prayer to God that summarizes your thoughts.

_____

_____

What are you going to do, say, or think today that will demonstrate obedience to God?

_____

_____

THOUGHT FOR THE DAY
Discipline is everything you do to train
your child in the way he should go.

DAY 5—MAKING DISCIPLES

Parenthood is the process of making disciples of your children. As Jesus walked this earth, He selected a dozen men, saying, "Follow me" (Matthew 10:1; compare 4:19). Before He went to the cross, He prayed:

"For I have given to them the words which You have given Me; and they have received them, and have known surely that I came forth from You; and they have believed that You sent Me. As you sent me into the world, I also have sent them into the world..
JOHN 17:8, 18

As you study the gospels, you realize that each of the disciples was an individual. Yet each one was given the same holy standard for daily living, the standard of the Lord Jesus.

In writing to the Philippians, Paul says:

But one thing I do...I press toward the goal for the prize of the upward call of God in Christ Jesus.
PHILIPPIANS 3;13, 14

Thus he takes upon himself the responsibility of being a living example.

Parents, too, should live as Paul did, striving for the same high calling. Fortunate is the child whose parents give him such a living example that he can safely follow in their footsteps. Fortunate is the child who has parents each of whom can say to him,

> *"Fortunate is the child whose parents give him such a living example that he can safely follow in their footsteps."*

The things which you learned and received and heard and saw in me, these do, and the God of peace will be with you.
PHILIPPIANS 4:9

The realization that your children could turn out to be the kind of person that you are ought to be a satisfying one. (Study Luke 6:40 and 1 Corinthians 11:1.)

Examine your life. Do your children want to be like you? Why? Do you want your children to be and act like you? Why?

_____

_____

_____

_____

Parents should teach their children by example and by words as did the Lord Jesus and Paul. Parents ought to be living models for their children. As someone has said, "The best way to teach character is to have it around the house."

> *"The best way to teach character is to have it around the house."*

When you go to school and study under a certain teacher, you follow him as your guide. He sets the way that you should go; and you become, in lesser or greater measure, his disciple. You learn from his information and absorb his basic philosophy. You may even acquire his physical mannerisms. Likewise, as parents, you should realize that your big job is to help your children go in the right direction.

It is obvious that, before you can help a child go where he should go, you must know where he should go.

What do you want to teach your children?

_____

_____

_____

You must be convinced that what you ask your children to do is worth doing. If you are not sure in your own mind that the thing you ask your children to do is worthwhile, you had better not ask him to do it. Somehow your children can sense insincerity and uncertainty in your eye or your gesture if present. It is easy to tell your son to be kind to your daughter if you are kind to your partner. You need to be practicing what you want your children to practice.

> *"You must be convinced that what you ask your children to do is worth doing."*

APPLICATION (OBEDIENCE TO GOD)

What did God teach me today:

_____

_____

Applying what God is pointing out to you is essential. How will you obey the Lord today?

_____

_____

Write a short prayer to God that summarizes your thoughts.

_____

_____

What are you going to do, say, or think today that will demonstrate obedience to God?

_____

_____

THOUGHT FOR THE DAY
The parent's greatest job is to know Christ and to train the children to be like Christ.

15

UNIT 2

RELAX AND HAVE FUN!

THOUGHT STARTER
God designed parenthood to be practiced by inexperienced parents.

MEMORY VERSE
Let your father and your mother be glad,
And let her who bore you rejoice.
PROVERBS 23:25

par·ent·ing
(pâr´en-tíng) (pár´-) —n. The rearing of a child or children, esp. the care, love, and guidance given by parents[2]

DAY 1—RELAX AND ENJOY YOUR CHILDREN

Writing about family living from my perch at age 76 is quite different from when we first wrote 30 years ago. There is one statement in a book quoted by Socrates in 469 B.C. It bears listening to today.

> If I could get to the highest place in Athens, I would lift up my voice and say, "What mean ye fellow citizens that you turn every stone to scrape wealth together and take so little care of your children, to whom you must one day relinquish it all?"

Sounds like a modern statement, doesn't it? Isn't it true that by the time you do your job, get in some recreation, and carry out your social opportunities, it becomes difficult to find time or energy to pay enough attention to your children?

If you spend a lot of time with your children, you'll learn a lot about them. You will also learn a lot about yourself.

If you spend a lot of time with your children, you will learn a lot about them. You will also learn a lot about yourself. You can always count on your children to pop the bubble—to shatter your polished image of yourself.

I can chuckle about it now. One of our preschool children taught us a lesson we never forgot. It was when we were privileged by a visit of our college president. It was quite an honor for a couple of young students to entertain the president, and we were determined to make the most of it.

The apartment looked as it had never looked before. Everything was in place, polished to a high luster. We were supposed to act as though it was always this way and carefully coached our little preschool children on what they could and couldn't say. We practically wrote them a script, but how painfully we paid for the sham we were creating.

So the president came. We stumbled over ourselves to make him comfortable. We got him to the table all right and sat him next to our little daughter who had barely learned to talk. That was a mistake. (It is interesting to note how many mistakes you can make when you are trying to put up a front.)

During the meal this little tot said to the president in her bird-like voice:
"Will you please pass the salt?"
Nobody paid any attention. We were listening to the president. So she tried again.
"Will you please pass the salt?" This small, little voice was easy to ignore as we strained at every word of the president.

The third time this little curly-haired tot single-handedly smashed all illusion about the offspring of the Brandt family we had so carefully constructed. She hammered our distinguished guest on the arm and yelled:

"Pass the salt or I'll knock your block off!"

> *"Pass the salt or I'll knock your block off!"*

What would you do if your preschooler did this?

_____

_____

_____

I turned all shades of angry purple. The most palatable idea to me at that moment was to twist that little kid into a pretzel. Yet there was no real reason to be angry. She had simply exposed my spirit—the spirit she had seen at previous meals. Also, we should have known we were expecting too much of a tiny child.

I have told this story all over the world and everyone thinks it is funny. Why didn't I think it was funny?

It would be great if we could enjoy our experiences as much as we enjoy talking about them! At the time it happened the incident seemed like a major catastrophe. Today it is an amusing incident.

> *It would be great if we could enjoy our experiences as much as we enjoy talking about them!*

18

RELAX AND HAVE FUN

APPLICATION (OBEDIENCE TO GOD)

What did God teach me today:

_____

_____

Applying what God is pointing out to you is essential. How will you obey the Lord today?

_____

_____

Write a short prayer to God that summarizes your thoughts.

_____

_____

What are you going to do, say, or think today that will demonstrate obedience to God?

_____

_____

THOUGHT FOR THE DAY
Relax and enjoy your children as they are.

DAY 2—THE SHADOW OF DEATH REVEALS LOVE

I had no idea how tender a father could feel toward his child until our little Beth developed viral pneumonia and passed under the shadow of death.

She had been crying a lot in her playpen. I accused my wife of spoiling her, but she insisted our baby was ill. We agreed to let the doctor decide. His terrible diagnosis of viral pneumonia left us weak with fear.

At the time there was no known treatment. We left her alone in the hospital, went home to wait, and wait.

Not only would she not respond, but she also got to the place where she would not eat. I stood helpless by the bedside of our little baby as she wasted away, and I then realized how much I loved that little youngster. A few days earlier I had been mad at her. Now with a heart filled with

"My wife and I clung to each other, desperately praying for the life of our baby."

love there was nothing I would not do for her. My wife and I clung to each other, desperately praying for the life of our baby. I asked God to forgive me for my impatience and lack of concern.

Have you experienced an event that revealed your love for your child/children? Why do you think you had to go through such events to reveal your love?

_____

_____

_____

_____

Day after day, I rushed from classes at the college to be with my daughter. Still she would not eat, so the attendants began feeding her intravenously. She continued to grow thinner and thinner.

One evening I asked the nurse if I could hold my little girl. That night Beth took some milk from the bottle as I held her in my arms. She would not eat for anyone else. Only I could feed her—I who had been angry with her for crying too much. I who had actually blocked taking her to a doctor because I though she was being "spoiled."

Finally, she recovered. We need to know and respect our children. The Bible states it this way:

"Whoever receives one of these little children in My name receives Me; and whoever receives Me, receives not Me but Him who sent Me."
MARK 9:37

I still smile at the time the same child discovered her shadow. She turned one way and it disappeared. Then it was back again. She could not run away from it. How do you explain a shadow?

When our son was a baby I put him in a basket suspended between the handlebars of my bicycle. One day he fell out of the basket as we pedaled along. What a shock. When I picked him up, he had a black eye and a bruised face. It hurt me as much as it hurt him. As I was trying to explain to my wife what happened, I dropped him again. At moments like these you realize how tenderly you can feel toward someone.

This is the same child who came to his mother with a puzzled look on his face and said, "Mom, how come I've got pipes in my arms?" How do you explain what a bone is?

When you have these experiences, a Biblical principle is easy to accept:

**Be kindly affectionate to one another with brotherly
love, in honor giving preference to one another.**
ROMANS 12:10

There is, however another side to living with children. Tomorrow's lesson will look at the other side.

APPLICATION (OBEDIENCE TO GOD)

What did God teach me today:

_____

_____

Applying what God is pointing out to you is essential. How will you obey the Lord today?

_____

_____

Write a short prayer to God that summarizes your thoughts.

_____

_____

What are you going to do, say, or think today that will demonstrate obedience to God?

_____

_____

THOUGHT FOR THE DAY
We need to know and respect our children.

DAY 3—RELAX—YOU'VE GOT TO BE KIDDING!

I remember one of my professors telling me, "Don't make parenting so difficult, just relax and have fun! Don't think you have to know everything in order to be a good parent."

It starts out as a dream. Doting, expectant fathers and their pregnant wives dream about the sweet little infant all

> *"Don't make parenting so difficult, just relax and have fun!"*

cozy in pink and blue blankets with ribbons and talcum powder. With smiles in their eyes, they turn to each other and vow. "We're going to be the best parents ever!"

Then the baby arrives. Suddenly the parents discover that "the dream" yells. And smells. And has a reversible stomach. All at 3 a.m.

Our baby cried and was often unable to be comforted. We got no slept little at night and very little during the day. My wife got up one night about 3 a.m. for about the fourth time! Still asleep, she picked up the little bundle and began patting it saying, "It's okay honey." To her surprise, she was holding a pillow that she had taken from the closet. Our baby was still in his bed screaming to the top of his lungs!

> *"I can remember taking our squalling baby and shoving it toward my wife, saying; "You take it."*

It's enough to make a grown man cry—or even worse. I can remember taking our squalling baby and shoving it toward my wife, saying;

"You take it."

It is humbling to realize that what you thought were wonderful, parental instincts can not always be counted on when you need them.

Why do you think some of your parental instincts are not as pleasant as you thought they would be?

_____

_____

_____

_____

Children

> Before I got married I had six theories about bringing up children; now I have six children, and no theories. John Wilmot Earl of Rochester (1647-1680)[3] —English courtier, poet.

Imagine a big man letting a tiny little baby make him angry! Yet it happens all the time.

Children's antics will stir up what is in your heart. If there is anger, impatience, selfishness, meanness, malice, cruelty, or partiality in the heart, children will bring it out of you. This is one of the benefits of having a family.

> *"Children's antics will stir up what is in your heart."*

Parenthood will keep you up to date on your spiritual condition.

> *Parenthood will keep you up to date on your spiritual condition.*

Can you remember the last time your child or someone else's child stirred up what was in your heart? Describe the situation below. What was your response?

_____

_____

_____

_____

APPLICATION (OBEDIENCE TO GOD)

What did God teach me today:

_____

_____

Applying what God is pointing out to you is essential. How will you obey the Lord today?

_____

_____

Write a short prayer to God that summarizes your thoughts.

_____

_____

What are you going to do, say, or think today that will demonstrate obedience to God?

_____

_____

THOUGHT FOR THE DAY
If you are not having fun as a parent,
check the condition of your heart.

DAY 4—CONFIDENT EXPECTATION

During my graduate work at Cornell University, the faculty experimented with different methods of helping children and parents. These were cleverly done. One well thought out series involved mothers who could not control their children. The incidents were recorded on film and then shown to various classes.

I will never forget the one about the mother who could not feed her son applesauce. Every time she tried, the boy shoved the spoon away. This was the cue for the mother to turn to the researcher and shrug.

"See? He just won't eat it."

The researcher told her to try again, which she did—unsuccessfully. Finally, the mother gave up.

"This happens all the time," the mother said.

Then one of the teachers tried it. She was determined in a gentle and firm way. She meant to feed that child applesauce—that was obvious.

That teacher put some applesauce on the spoon, headed it toward the child's mouth, and the child shoved it aside.

Without any hesitation, the teacher brought the spoon back and into the child's mouth.

Gulp! One spoonful of applesauce down the hatch. The child was surprised. The mother even more so.

The teacher did it again. This time the child was ready and pushed the spoon away, but the teacher again steadily returned the spoon back and around the little fist. Once more, the applesauce popped into the child's mouth.

Another surprised gulp. Now the child had two spoonfuls of applesauce in his stomach.

A third thrust with the spoon again succeeded. The fourth thrust went in without any resistance at all.

Soon the child was enjoying the applesauce more than the hitting. In no time at all the teacher had emptied the entire dish of applesauce—a spoon at a time—into the child's now willing mouth.

What do you see as the difference between the teacher and parent's method?

_____

_____

_____

_____

Why The Difference?

There were two reasons. First, a handy tool called **confident expectation.**

This assumes that you are doing or requiring something you believe is in the best interests of the child. If you are you will have enough conviction to see it through.

Second, in addition to wanting to do the child a favor, the teacher's manner was friendly, gentle, and firm.

The teacher explained this to the stunned mother. It was a simple matter. The mother expected to fail. She was taking her cues from that little child. A little bit of resistance (which is normal in human beings) from the small child was enough to frustrate a grown woman.

"Confident expectation assumes that you are doing or requiring something you believe is in the best interests of the child."

Does resistance from children or adults frustrate you the most? Why?

_____

_____

_____

In the next few sessions the mother watched the teacher successfully feed bowl after bowl of applesauce to her child. One thing was obvious in all the sessions. The teacher was not forcing the applesauce into the child's mouth just to prove a point. She wanted to do the child a favor. Her manner was friendly, gentle, and firm.

"Resistance can be overcome with gentle, well-founded pressure—pressure that is based on confident expectation."

The teacher taught the mother that resistance is to be expected from children but that it can be overcome with gentle, well-founded pressure—pressure that is based on confident expectation.

After a few days of observing, the mother was urged to try again. The child took one look at the setup—the bowl of applesauce...the spoon...the mother. It all came back to him. He knew his role in this drama. Resist.

However, he was up against someone different. This time, the mother was dedicated to success. She was convinced she was doing the child a favor.

She took a spoonful of applesauce and headed it for the child. Ah hah! You could see the child's thinking mirrored on his face. He batted it away.

The mother brought it back. With a gleam in his eye, the child shoved it aside. This time she brought it back quicker than he expected and the spoonful of applesauce disappeared into his pouting mouth.

Gulp, indeed. The child could not believe his taste buds. The betrayed expression on his face was a sight to see.

The mother's expression was incredible. You would have thought she had just inherited a million dollars. Her face was wreathed in a million dollar glow of triumph.

She was victorious! She had placed a spoonful of applesauce into her child's mouth. Soon, the child sensed the difference, too. His mother's manner was friendly, gentle, and firm. Before the bowl was empty the scene changed to a mother feeding applesauce to a willing and cooperative child.

Remember that phrase…confident expectation. If you are to give your children the guidance they need, it will first of all take conviction on your part that you truly are doing your children a favor by what you are asking them to do.

APPLICATION (OBEDIENCE TO GOD)

What did God teach me today:

_____

_____

Applying what God is pointing out to you is essential. How will you obey the Lord today?

_____

_____

Write a short prayer to God that summarizes your thoughts.

_____

_____

What are you going to do, say, or think today that will demonstrate obedience to God?

_____

_____

THOUGHT FOR THE DAY
Expect success. Parenting will be a lot more fun.

DAY 5—ME, AN AUTHORITY?

Success, however, implies wisdom from God and a knowledge of your child. You can be the world's greatest authority on the subject of your children—if you pay attention to them.

And, of course, that's the catch. You must work at it—talk with them. Listen to them. Play with them. Read to them. Pray with them. Work with them.

Spend time with them.

Do it.

Become an authority on your children.

Examine your own relationship with your child/children. If a friend asked about your relationship, how would you describe it?

_____

_____

_____

Parents play a strategic role in society—to put it more correctly, the most strategic role in society.

You might say it is over for us this matter of being parents. At least we have raised all our children to the point where they are out on their own.

I am not saying that because we did not like the job. I am saying it because every one of us who has children realizes that there is an element of suspense in raising children. How will they turn out?

The principles in this book are the same ones my wife and I used when our children were quite small. They worked for us—and for thousands of parents who have consulted with me.

> *I want to say that this is the stage I like the most.*
> *"...there is an element of suspense in raising children."*

These principles made those years of parenthood a pleasant time. Parenthood should be enjoyable; even during those years we fear the most. The teenage years, for example, can be the greatest of all.

> *"Never forget that the One who knows your child's needs better than you is Jesus Christ."*

Parenthood is not difficult. It is demanding. It takes time, some deep convictions, your own good example, some knowledge of your kids, following the teachings of the Bible, and a loving spirit. Never forget that the One who knows your child's needs better than you is Jesus Christ. He knows things you do not know and when you have a close relationship with Him, you will know the truth about your child.

27

**"Call to Me and I will answer you, and show you great
and mighty things, which you do not know.**
JEREMIAH 33:3

**"If you abide in My word, you are my disciples indeed.
And you shall know the truth, and the truth shall make you free."**
JOHN 8:31-32

Parents are strategic, important people, involved in one of the greatest adventures of life. Never let go of the dream about being the best parents ever.

You can expect success—and also learn from your children. Expect to grow, to change, and to improve.

APPLICATION (OBEDIENCE TO GOD)

What did God teach me today:

_____

_____

Applying what God is pointing out to you is essential. How will you obey the Lord today?

_____

_____

Write a short prayer to God that summarizes your thoughts.

_____

_____

What are you going to do, say, or think today that will demonstrate obedience to God?

_____

_____

THOUGHT FOR THE DAY
Become an authority on your child by getting
to know him better than anyone else knows him.

UNIT 3

I'M NOT HAVING FUN YET!

THOUGHT STARTER

Considering others better than yourself is a good start to good parenting.

MEMORY VERSE

**Let each of you look out not only for his own interests,
but also for the interests of others.**

PHILIPPIANS 2:4

DAY 1—I PLANNED TO BE A "GOOD" PARENT

Let's have fun. Expect success. Learn as you "parent." Develop meaningful relationships.

These are all good exciting phrases. They describe what every parent really wants. They must be central to your adventure into enjoyable parenthood. For a moment though, let's digress. Let's look at some parents who aren't having fun.

Why get into the negative? Simple. Because most parents are not having fun.

> "Why get into the negative? Simple. Because most parents are not having fun."

Conflict Between Parents

Perry Manning's folks fought nearly every day over something he did or wanted to do. So he figured it was just another battle of words when they squared off on the issue of his car.

"That boy is a menace on the road," he heard his mother say.

"He'll mature," replied his dad.

"But half the time we don't know where he is," his mother cut in.

"Well, you can't fence in a seventeen-year-old," his dad said.

Then Perry heard them pick up their long-standing quarrel over what Christian training is and is not. He knew they would come to no conclusion, and while they were postponing a decision about him he would go on doing what he wanted to do.

All during their time of haggling and indecisiveness over his behavior, Perry collected a few traffic tickets and found a buddy to bump out fenders. After his graduation, he was out almost every night. He dated a girl whose reputation was questionable.

If friends of yours had a son like this and came to you for help, how would you help them?

_____

_____

_____

"Oh, don't worry about Perry and that girl," his dad said to his mother. "I went with five girls before I met you. I'll put a stop to this nonsense," he said. Quickly he planned a trip to Yellowstone. Perry drove with his parents. The day he became of legal age he caught a bus for home.

The Mannings returned home, too—straight to the Christian Counseling Clinic to see what they could do about their son.

"There's nothing you can do," I said to the two tearful parents, "except to pray to God that your boy will come to his senses."

They had relinquished control of their son when they failed to agree on how to raise him. The spirit of conflict between mother and father prevented the exercise of any parental judgment. How different things would have been had they practiced:

Now I plead with you, brethren, by the name of our Lord Jesus Christ, that you all speak the same thing, and that there be no divisions among you, but that you be perfectly joined together in the same mind and in the same judgment.
1 CORINTHIANS 1:10

Somehow, they could not find an answer to Perry's searching question the day he left them. He asked, "If what I'm doing at eighteen is so terrible, why wasn't it bad enough to stop me at seventeen?"

The Bible says to, "train up a child in the way he should go, and when he is old he will not depart from it." (Proverbs 22:6). The Bible further states,

Be kindly affectionate to one another with brotherly love, in honor giving preference to one another.
ROMANS 12:10

If these truths are applied to parenthood, the way a child should go becomes a matter of parental decision, with a foundation of affection between the parents and toward the children. Parents quickly discover that children tend to go their own way, just as they themselves do.

> *The demands of parenthood expose the soul. They reveal the quality of the marriage partnership and the character of each parent.*

The demands of parenthood expose the soul. They reveal the quality of the marriage partnership and the character of each parent.

A common pattern is brought out in the counseling of parents who have difficulty with their children. A pattern usually develops that one or both parents are irritated by the child. The parents generally differ over what the limits should be, over how to deal with the child's resistance, or over the pattern of supervision. In brief, the problem is most often one of the marriage relationship rather than one between parent and child.

So we leave the discussion about the child and turn to an examination of the marriage. The parents are divided and are reacting toward each other with some form of selfishness. This brings us right back to the individual. Each can, if he chooses, repent of his selfishness and irritability and receive forgiveness from God. Each may have a change of heart for the asking. The marriage relationship can then be restored. In a spirit of kindly affection toward each other, the parents can resolve the issues over limits and patterns of supervision, and methods of dealing with the child's resistance. The changed heart will also enable the parent to deal with the child firmly but without malice.

APPLICATION (OBEDIENCE TO GOD)

What did God teach me today:

_____

_____

Applying what God is pointing out to you is essential. How will you obey the Lord today?

_____

_____

Write a short prayer to God that summarizes your thoughts.

_____

_____

What are you going to do, say, or think today that will demonstrate obedience to God?

_____

_____

THOUGHT FOR THE DAY

Agree with one another so that there may be no divisions among you and that you may be perfectly united in mind and thought.

DAY 2—THE IDEAL FAMILY

Sensible couples start out planning for their relationship to be the best ever. In all my years of counseling, I have never had one parent or set of parents come to me and say, "Well, here we are, Dr. Brandt. We are bursting with mutual admiration because we've succeeded at reaching our goal. Our objective was to create an intolerable situation for the two of us and our children."

"Now we've done it—created the perfect mess. We can't stand each other. We've ruined a good relationship—exactly what we started out to do."

Of course that is not what they intended. People just do not set such goals. Well, why is this marital upheaval in our society happening? Many good people start marriage with the highest of hopes and end up hopelessly at odds. The idea of personal freedom becomes an obsession and marriage and parenthood becomes a nightmare with no apparent solution.

> *"Many good people start marriage with the highest of hopes and end up hopelessly at odds."*

Jesus approached this attitude in the Bible by saying:

"If anyone desires to come after Me, let him deny himself..."
LUKE 9:23

The demands of parenting will force the parent to make some choices. They will either turn Godward for a change of heart or they will struggle with an irritable spirit.

Many parents attempt to deal with their children by simply avoiding conflict. If there is a possible clash of opinions, they avoid it. After all, it is important to give our children the freedom to make their own decisions, isn't it? Consider a mother comes into her child's room in the morning, rouses her, and the following dialogue ensues:

Mother: Well, shall we get up today?

Child: No. (Child closes her eyes and burrows back down under the covers.)

Mother: You have to get up to put your dress on. You do want to get dressed, don't you?

Child: No. (Child snuggles down tighter than ever pulling a pillow over her head.)

Mother: You can eat breakfast after you put your dress on. You'd like to do that, wouldn't you?

Child: (A sound emerges from underneath the pillow that could be translated only as another No.)

Mother: After breakfast, you can watch TV. You'd like that, wouldn't you?

Child: (No answer at all, now.)

And so it goes. Every morning this mother goes through the same twenty-minute nerve wracking ritual as she cajoles her child into getting up for another day. The mother does this for the one simple reason—that she wants to avoid conflicts in life. However, forcing a child to do certain things results in conflicts and resistance.

Why do you think parents want to avoid conflicts and resistance in their children?

_____

_____

Parents go through a similar agony in other situations, passing along the decisions to the child, "Shall we make our bed and pick up our room? Shall we eat breakfast? Shall we drink our milk? Shall we go to school? Aren't you staying out too late? Aren't you running with the wrong crowd?" And the daily fight is on.

The Nightmare

One lady described to me a completely fruitless dialogue that had become an everyday occurrence at home with her thirteen-year-old son.

Mother: It's time to take out the garbage.

Son: (No response)

Mother: (irritated) I said it's time to take out the garbage!

Son: All right…all right.

Mother: (Angry and losing control) Well, don't just stand there! I said Take out the garbage!

Finally, the son stirs and goes through the evening ritual of taking out the garbage. As usual, he leaves one sack. Then he sits down again.

Mother: (Now screaming) You stupid, rebellious kid! Get the rest of that garbage and take it out…and don't try to tell me you didn't see…

It is easy to see why the woman felt as she did when she came to my office.

"I just hate myself. I'm turning into a mess. I'm just nothing but a screaming, old nag of a mother."

Children's antics will stir up what is in your heart. If there is anger, impatience, selfishness, meanness, malice, cruelty, or partiality in the heart, children will bring it out of you. This is one of the benefits of having a family. Parenthood will keep you up to date on your spiritual condition.

To compound their plight, parenthood is a twenty-year process.

For some parents this is good news. For most, this is a scary thought. You mean I have to put up with the screaming…the disobedience…the lack of respect…the rebellion for twenty years?

Is that all I have to look forward to?

Maybe. In any case, it is about twenty years per child. If you have more than one, it is much longer.

Sounds like a sentence, doesn't it? Almost as if the gavel had slammed down and the judge had said: "I sentence you to twenty years in parenthood."

No wonder many people want to run away.

> *"I sentence you to twenty years in parenthood."*

APPLICATION (OBEDIENCE TO GOD)

What did God teach me today:

_____

_____

Applying what God is pointing out to you is essential. How will you obey the Lord today?

_____

_____

Write a short prayer to God that summarizes your thoughts.

_____

_____

What are you going to do, say, or think today that will demonstrate obedience to God?

_____

_____

THOUGHT FOR THE DAY
People do not start their parenting days dreaming up ways they can be "bad" parents.

DAY 3—FAMILY FAILURES

Are we perpetrating a hoax by saying that parenthood ought to be a lot of fun? Is that unrealistic? A pie in the sky suggestion?

I guess one thing we can agree on—parenthood definitely will bring out the worst in us. We may not like what we see. At the office we can look good most of the time. In the club or other organization we can appear pretty much in control. You cannot pretend twenty-four hours a day. So parenthood will not let you hide the worst side of yourself.

It is scary. We would rather not see our fault mirrored in our children's lives.

Training By Example

When Mrs. Greene wanted to move and her husband did not, she managed to find so much fault with the house that the family ended up moving.

Mr. Greene thought they could not afford a new carpet, but his wife proved they could. She talked her husband into installing an extension phone for their daughter, Laurie. When Mrs. Greene wanted to exchange a long-planned camping trip for the World's Fair, she pouted until everyone came around to her view.

Mrs. Greene did not appear to be a demanding woman. Appearances aside, with full consciousness of her methods, she imposed her will on others, either subtly or directly.

Teen-age Laurie seemed to go her own way, knowing her father could be ignored and having learned how to work around her mother's dominance. Her wants were seldom out of line, so there were few conflicts—until Ray came along.

Is this family destined for failure? State why you believe it is or is not.

_____

_____

_____

"Raymond isn't good enough for you," Mrs. Greene proclaimed.

"Why do you say that?"

"He's not a Christian," her mother replied. "And he'll never hold down a decent job."

"We love each other," insisted Laurie.

Her persuasion ineffective, Mrs. Greene flatly told Laurie she was not to see Ray anymore.

"But I will! I will!" screamed Laurie.

Mrs. Greene brought to bear every device she had ever used to control a situation. She cried; she threatened; she went to bed with sick headaches; she tried shaming Laurie; and she told Ray she did not approve of him. Laurie refused to budge.

Mrs. Greene asked her husband for help. But long ago he had learned to be neutral. Then she came to our clinic, asking us to make Laurie see the error of her way.

After we heard the story, our advice to Mrs. Greene was, "You seem to have forgotten the truth of God's Word."

> **Do not be deceived, God is not mocked; for**
> **whatever a man sows, that he will also reap.**
> GALATIANS 6:7

You have trained your daughter well by your example of getting what you want, in any way that it takes to get it. You are seeing yourself reproduced in Laurie—a selfishly demanding, determined, stubborn girl."

You have molded her in your own image. Only God can break the mold. You will just have to wait to see if, in spite of you, He does.

It takes thirteen years for a child to reach the teens. This may strike you as an obvious statement, and it is. It is also a reminder that the teen years do not sneak up on you. Thirteen years is a long time, and the relationship established between parents and children during this time will have much to do with the way the teen years will be managed.

God will have touched the heart of parents many times to pray for their children in those thirteen years. The sad fact is that many parents do not take the time to pray for their children until the children are adults. Prayerlessness on the part of parents will leave its mark.

> *Prayerlessness on the part of parents will leave its mark.*

During this time the parents should learn to work together happily as a team. They have come to a meeting of the minds on the management of the children. By now they have firm convictions on the way the children should go. They have developed a set of limits and have learned to adjust them along the way. They have learned to deal with the resistance of their children and have developed a pattern of effective supervision.

The Bible makes some statements that are debated by parents and sociologists. For example,

> **Correct your son, and he will give you rest;**
> **Yes, he will give delight to your soul.**
> PROVERBS 29:17

And a warning,

The rod and reproof give wisdom, But a child left to himself, brings shame to his mother.
PROVERBS 29:15

By the time a child reaches the teens, his parents will have had ample time to test these admonitions and to develop some firm convictions about the need to train, to correct, and to supervise.

On the other hand, if parents remain divided on these issues, the growing resistance to limits in the teen years will bring these uncertainties and divisions to light. Parents will fail to act either for lack of firm conviction or for being divided.

The experiences set forth here make it clear that teen-agers will not respect parents who are divided and without convictions. As parents resolve their differences and demonstrate that their convictions and guidelines have served them well, they will regain the respect and cooperation of their children.

APPLICATION (OBEDIENCE TO GOD)

What did God teach me today:

_____

_____

Applying what God is pointing out to you is essential. How will you obey the Lord today?

_____

_____

Write a short prayer to God that summarizes your thoughts.

_____

_____

What are you going to do, say, or think today that will demonstrate obedience to God?

_____

_____

THOUGHT FOR THE DAY
Two Spirit-filled parents will encourage opportunities for "good" families to develop.

DAY 4—FAMILY RESCUE NEEDED!

A swimming teacher was describing how to properly rescue a drowning person. As I listened I was fascinated by the little known precautionary step called the quick reverse.

"The quick reverse," said the teacher, "is used when the rescuer comes close to the victim, which is the moment of greatest potential danger.

"A drowning victim is desperate and irrational. If he can, he will grab the lifesaver, immobilize, or even drown him.

"A good quick reverse stops the rescuer's momentum before he gets hopelessly and fatally trapped. It also moves the lifesaver out of the victim's reach.

"The lifesaver doesn't abandon the victim. The quick reverse enables the rescuer to calmly study the victim, approach the victim safely, take charge, and tow him to safety.

"A knowledgeable rescuer does not panic, regardless of the victim's behavior. He takes command, acts decisively (even if the victim struggles against him), and helps the victim reach a common goal: SAFETY.

"A good lifesaver is not afraid of people in trouble. It is his job to rescue them. It gives him satisfaction.

"Nor does a good lifesaver dive in every time he sees someone struggling. He does not tamper with the child who is just learning how to swim and struggling along the side of the pool. It is important for that child to be allowed to work on the problem himself.

"A good lifesaver gets involved only when there's trouble brewing. He has to be calm, happy, cooperative, able, under control, and trained.

"If he is not, a crisis situation will cause him to panic. He might run away from it; completely deserting the pool he has agreed to guard. He might also swim out and realize he is incapable of rescue and let the victim sink.

"Or he might swim right into the arms of danger, get grabbed by the victim and end up part of a double drowning."

To some of us, the teacher's speech may seem highly technical. Notice how it parallels parenthood. Just like the swimmers at a pool, children in a family situation are looking for fun out of life...pleasure...fellowship...good health.

Yet sometimes they get into trouble. Just like the swimmer who gets in trouble, the child does not plan to drown. He simply lacks knowledge. Maybe he is unprepared, lacks ability or training, ignores obvious dangers, or disobeys the rules.

Regardless, when a child is drowning in life's problems, he needs to be rescued. He needs a capable "lifesaver" to come after him and tow him to safety. He needs a parent who is ready to move in at the first sign of danger.

Yet, many children are not rescued. Their parents are in no position to help. They are either out of control themselves, have no plan, or also are sinking.

> "Untrained parents are in a position of weakness and are trapped in a never ending series of crises."

Untrained parents are in a position of weakness and are trapped in a never ending series of crises. They seem unable to change their direction and have no idea of any alternatives—except maybe to run off and get a divorce and let their children "drown." Otherwise, they would drown too.

Their lives need a quick reverse.

Short-Lived Vow

Serious parents do not wake up in the morning planning to make his child's life miserable. No parent vows each morning: "Today, I'm going to be grumpy, crabby, and impossible."

Can you imagine approaching parenthood with this attitude? Imagine you are in a maternity waiting room with an expectant father. Suddenly the father to be looks up at the ceiling and says with a strong tinge of iron-willed determination, "Boy-oh-boy, this baby is going to regret having me as a father. I'm going to draw on all the ingenuity and creativity possible to make this little tike's life utterly miserable."

> No parent vows each morning: "Today, I'm going to be grumpy, crabby, and impossible."

No. It does not work that way. When the alarm goes off, it is just the opposite.

"Today will be different," the mother vows. "A great day. No screaming—impatient orders—arguing."

As Mom is making her vow, a situation is developing that will easily crush that well-meaning vow. In the hall outside the bathroom, her son is beating on the door.

"Hey, who's in there? You've been tying up the bathroom for half an hour. Do you think you're the only one who has to go to school?"

"Oh, buzz off!" comes the answer from big sister. "If you want to use the bathroom, why don't you go down in the basement and use the bathroom down there?"

"Why should I always have to be the one who uses the basement bathroom? Come on, now, open up. Now! Or I'll tell Mom!" This threat is accompanied by a drum roll on the door. Just then Mother comes on the scene.

She finds herself in the middle of a battle between a child who wants to use the bathroom and another who has locked herself in.

It does not take her long to get into the controversy. Several screams, protestations, and mutterings later she has settled the controversy, but she is irritated and upset.

Yet…only minutes before…she had vowed that this would be a perfect day. Write the last time you remember something like this happening in your house.

_____

_____

_____

How did you respond?

_____

_____

How did your children respond?

_____

_____

Dad Gets Involved Too

Often the same happens for the well intentioned dad. Just before he pulls into the driveway coming home from work, he vows, "Tonight I'm not going to be a grouch. Tonight I'm going to have fun with the family."

> "Tonight I'm not going to be a grouch. Tonight I'm going to have fun with the family."

Suddenly he finds his way blocked by two bicycles parked in the driveway, inspite of his many lectures against such a situation.

He parks the car, the engine running, halfway in the driveway and halfway in the street, slams the door, and runs toward the house.

Dad is hardly in the door before he is after everyone in sight.

"How many times do I have to tell you guys…Get those bicycles out of the driveway! How am I going to park the car?"

He's out of control—just making noise without getting any facts. He continues yelling, turning now on his wife. Without one loving gesture or question, he lays her out too. "I thought I made it clear that bicycles should not be parked in the driveway." And the fight is on…

The mom at breakfast…the father coming home from work. Both found themselves in a crisis situation. They blew the rescue, didn't they?

We are looking for the cause of the awful feelings and unbelievable behavior experienced around your partner and children—the people you want to love and be decent toward.

In other words, you have missed the mark.

What mark?

In the consulting room everyone expresses the same basic longings, the same goals—or mark—that all are shooting for:

1. To enjoy life everyday.
2. Obtain peace which will keep your thoughts and hearts quiet and at rest.
3. Increase in love toward one another.
4. Be unselfish and considerate.

Do you believe this is an impossible dream? If so, it is extremely critical that you think about and write down the reasons why. Think a few minutes and write your thoughts here:

_____

_____

_____

_____

_____

Would you be surprised if I told you that this is not an impossible dream? These attributes can characterize your life. They do not represent some distant, unreachable oasis.

Are you interested? Tomorrow you will examine the cure.

APPLICATION (OBEDIENCE TO GOD)

What did God teach me today:

_____

_____

Applying what God is pointing out to you is essential. How will you obey the Lord today?

_____

_____

Write a short prayer to God that summarizes your thoughts.

_____

_____

What are you going to do, say, or think today that will demonstrate obedience to God?

_____

_____

THOUGHT FOR THE DAY
Stay in touch with the life of your child.

DAY 5—THE BEGINNING OF THE "FAMILY CURE."

Now to examine the problem, the cause, and cure for your unhappiness.

But first—a warning!

I have watched many people explode with rage when I tried to explain the reasons for this behavior. I mention this only to warn you ahead of time that my answer comes from a source you may have rejected—the Bible—God's Word.

"Don't give me that Bible stuff!" shouted one of my clients. "I've had that crammed down my throat ever since I was a kid."

Yet, after listening and obeying what God said in His Word, this man saw his life turned around. He followed steps that have meant new life and happy parenthood for many.

For example, did you know that what you want for yourself (joy, peace, love, unselfishness, being considerate) is described in the Bible as God's will for you?

Still with me?

Let's start with the first questions...Why do I act the way I do? Why do I miss the mark?

The problem. The Bible describes your condition in two lines:

For the good that I will to do, I do not do; but the evil
I will not to do, that I practice.
ROMANS 7:19

This is the problem. Everyone misses the mark. Maybe you are one of the many who vowed that your marriage would be the greatest. Now you would settle for getting through breakfast without a squabble. You cannot control yourself, can you?

Cause. There is a mysterious stranger within you who will not behave as you intend to behave. The Bible describes the problem and provides a cause:

Now if I do what I will not to do, it is no longer I who do it,
but sin that dwells in me.
ROMANS 7:20

Did I use the wrong word? It is an ugly word in a sense. Before you dismiss it, think a minute. If I had said virus or cancer, you would listen. So, let's take another look at this definition of sin:

For the good that I will to do, I do not do; but the evil
I will not to do, that I practice.
ROMANS 7:19

Can you improve on this description of yourself? See if you can write an accurate description of how you respond to people and events.

_____

_____

_____

Even though you may not like the word sin, it is an accurate description. Do not get hung up on the word and miss some very important truths.

There is none who does good, no, not one.
ROMANS 3:12

"What do you mean, I've never done any good? I've done a lot of good in my life," you say.

You may be right. You have had many happy moments with your wife and children. You have been generous to others, and you may continue to be.

That is not the problem. If you were in a fit of temper or resentment or selfishness, no one could make you do today what you did for them yesterday. This is the problem.

We are all sunk if peace of mind depends upon someone else's choices, behavior, or moods. No, we are all in the same boat. We find ourselves powerless to exude joy, peace, gentleness in the face of a yelling husband, a pouting wife, bathroom fights, bicycles in the driveway, smelly diapers, or squalling babies.

> _"If you were in a fit of temper or resentment or selfishness, no one could make you do today what you did for them yesterday."_

The Joy Machine Is Missing

So you do not have a joy machine that kicks in when you need it like your air conditioner does? Do not be dismayed. You are not alone. This is how God's Word has described us for centuries. Marriage and parenthood just bring the condition out more dramatically.

At this point you may be thinking, "I've got marriage and family problems, and now he makes me out a sinner, too. This just compounds my problem with guilt."

> _"Marriage and parenthood just bring the condition out more dramatically."_

43

Granted. The diagnosis of sin may startle or even frighten you. It is like hearing your physician tell you an operation is needed. You are stunned, afraid, and unbelieving. You wish the problem would go away.

The physician does not give you the news to complicate your problems. His objective is to heal you, to correct something that is wrong. You are not functioning as you should or would because you are sick.

My goal for you is also your healing. The diagnosis of sin may be repulsive and frightening. But because you are not functioning as you should or would, your sin is revealed. Do not let the diagnosis scare you. There is a cure.

The Cure

God has a plan to save you from yourself, from your sins. You have everything to gain and nothing to lose from Him. The Bible says God will do for you what you cannot do for yourself. For instance:

> **And may the Lord make you increase and abound in love to one another and to all, just as we do to you.**
> 1 THESSALONIANS 3:12

This is what you are looking for. Let God give you what He has promised. Your reactions toward your partner and your children will change. The Bible describes the problem and defines the cause to a solution:

> **O wretched man that I am! Who will deliver me from this body of death? I thank God—through Jesus Christ our Lord!**
> ROMANS 7:24, 25

This is a name that sometimes makes people see red—Jesus Christ. People sometimes associate Him with unreasonable demands, punishment, or guilt. But let Him speak for Himself.

> **"For God did not send His Son into the world to condemn the world, but that the world through Him might be saved.**
> JOHN 3:17

Saved from what? Your nastiness, of course. Your sins. A sinner is like a traffic violator who has broken a traffic law. Nothing can change the fact that he is a violator. We have all experienced the sense of relief when we get out of a twenty mph traffic zone when we were traveling at forty mph.

You feel the same tension when you miss a mark of your own. You are vaguely aware of violating something, but what do you do about it? You must cure your problem through Jesus Christ. It is said of Him:

> **…you shall call His name Jesus, for He will save His people from their sins.**
> MATTHEW 1:21

It is Jesus who said:

"I am the way, the truth, and the life. No one comes to
the Father except through Me."
JOHN 14:6

"Behold, I stand at the door and knock. If anyone hears My voice and opens the
door, I will come in to him and dine with him, and he with Me.
REVELATION 3:20

How, then, do you approach God?

1. You start by recognizing that missing the mark is sin. You agree with God. Your sins have separated you from Him.

2. Next comes faith. There is only one way to approach God and that is to try it. Choose to believe in God and act on that belief.

3. Trust Jesus as your Savior. You can do this right now through prayer (prayer is talking with God). Here is a sample prayer:

"Lord Jesus, I need You. I open the door of my life and receive You as
my Savior and Lord. Thank You for forgiving my sins. Take control
of my life. Make me the kind of person You want me to be."

4. Confess your sins.

If we confess our sins, He is faithful and just to forgive us
our sins and to cleanse us from all unrighteousness.
1 JOHN 1:9

It's like, "Oops. I am going forty in a twenty mph zone. So I will acknowledge the fact that I am violating a law and need to change. I will simply take my foot off the accelerator and ask God for forgiveness."

Of course, repentance is involved. You have changed your mind about being a violator. You agree with the sign that you are violating a rule. This is what confession is. You admit you are wrong and plan to change.

When you do this, Jesus will forgive you and cleanse your life of those uncontrollable habits.

Why not try it? God can change your reactions to life. He can give you the resource you need. This is the quick reverse. This is the first step to enjoyable parenthood. Repeat step 4 as often as necessary.

If you are a Christian, but have neglected step 4, list your sins here and bring them to God. Ask Him to forgive you and cleane you. People have a vague idea of what sin is. On the chart following, spirit-filled living is compared to sin-controlled living. This chart may help you answer this question.

_____

_____

_____

_____

_____

You can use the following chart like a mirror. On the left hand side are the qualities that God will help you develop. On the right hand side is a list of sins. Check up on yourself as you do when you use a mirror to check up on your body.

Note: (The chart is based on Mark 7:21-23, Romans 1:28-31, Galatians 5:19-21, Ephesians 4:25-31, and 2 Timothy 3:1-5)

SPIRIT-CONTROLLED LIVING VS. SIN-CONTROLLED LIVING

SPIRIT-FILLED MIND

forgiveness	humility		
hope	thankfulness		
appreciation	confidence		
willingness	wisdom		
impartiality	faithful		
self-control	gratitude		
merciful			

SINS OF THE MIND

unforgiveness	pride
evil thoughts	ingratitude
covetousness	selfish ambition
greed	deceitfulness
lust	heartless
arrogance	faithless
senseless	haughty
despiteful	

SPIRIT-FILLED EMOTIONS

love	joy
peace	long-suffering
gentle spirit	kindly spirit
gladness	patient
	compassion

SINFUL EMOTIONS

hatred	anger
rebellion	unloving attitude
bitterness	jealousy
envy	malice
bad temper	rage

SPIRIT-FILLED MOUTH

truthfulness	praise
thankfulness	timeliness
gentle answer	soothing tongue
encouraging	pleasant words
tact	

SINS OF THE MOUTH

lying	slandering
complaining	disputing
yelling	backbiting
contentiousness	quarrelsomeness
boasting	blasphemy
gossip	

SPIRIT-FILLED BEHAVIOR

kindness	gentleness
righteousness	self-control
obedience	cooperation
goodness	sincerity
courage	servant
endurance	submissive
considerate	impartial

SINS OF BEHAVIOR

fornication	brutality
adultery	without self-control
drunkenness	stealing
murder	violence
revelry	disobedience to parents
insolent	brawling
ruthless	favoritism
factious	

Quick Reverse "Backlash"

One word of caution for you who decide you need a quick reverse and have decided to make a permanent relationship with Jesus Christ. That caution—expect your partner and/or children to be confused if you suddenly reverse your life.

A business friend of mine recently took the same step you have just taken. Noticing a difference in his life, his wife asked him what had happened. When he said he had asked Jesus Christ to take charge of his life, she shook her head and muttered, "Religion, eh? You'll get over it. It was the American Legion last year…the Boy Scouts the year before…it's just another one of your little excursions."

This is a natural reaction. Expect it. Give your family six months to be skeptical. Do not try to overwhelm them with your new approach to life. Just let it be natural. They will get the point.

APPLICATION (OBEDIENCE TO GOD)

What did God teach me today:

_____

_____

Applying what God is pointing out to you is essential. How will you obey the Lord today?

_____

_____

Write a short prayer to God that summarizes your thoughts.

_____

_____

What are you going to do, say, or think today that will demonstrate obedience to God?

_____

_____

THOUGHT FOR THE DAY
Jesus Christ is the cure for all your family problems.

UNIT 4
PARTNERS, NOT OPPONENTS!

THOUGHT STARTER
Husband and wife can choose to be partners or opponents,
but opponents can not be effective parents.

MEMORY VERSE
Submitting to one another in the fear of God.
EPHESIANS 5:21

DAY 1—PARENT PARTNERSHIP

Doesn't the word "partners" have a pleasant ring to it?

It reminds me of some other nice words: harmony…together…cooperation…agreement…appreciation…respect…success.

Any partnership is entered into with high hopes. It is hoped the partners will combine their resources, talents, and abilities, and will experience satisfaction and success in the process.

Can you imagine people who hate each other, do not trust one another, or who know ahead of time that they can not get along forming a partnership?

Do you know of a partnership that was formed for the purpose of lying, cheating, and fighting with each other? What would be their purpose?

_____

_____

_____

Can you imagine a partnership being formed with the hope that somewhere along the line the individuals involved will take each other to court and end up as frustrated enemies? This is done, of course. Who would say this is a sensible reason for forming one?

Obviously for a partnership to succeed, it takes honest people of good will who anticipate pleasant, happy relationships as they work together toward a common goal.

49

It is easy to understand a business partnership. For example, four men agree to form a partnership to build some apartment houses. Between them, they must achieve the following:

1. A credit rating good enough to get money.
2. A set of building plans
3. Acquire property.
4. Construct the building.
5. Manage the building.
6. Handle the income.

This is not a complete list, but it shows that a partnership requires resources, talent, cooperation, and agreement. Assuming honest men of good will, the project should give them a great deal of satisfaction and a sense of success. In Biblical language, it goes like this:

Fulfill my joy by being like-minded, having the same love, being of one accord, of one mind. Let nothing be done through selfish ambition or conceit, but in lowliness of mind let each esteem others better than himself.
PHILIPPIANS 2:2, 3

It is a simple matter to form a partnership. Making it achieve its objective is not so simple. That takes a lot of hard work. To do it in the spirit described in these Bible verses is a miracle.

> *"It is a simple matter to form a partnership. Making it achieve its objective is not so simple."*

Parenthood Is A Partnership

Obviously, the purpose of parenthood is to raise mature, happy purposeful adults. It does not matter whether parents are in the business voluntarily or involuntarily. The children are there. They will not dissolve. So the parents' task is to combine their own resources, talents, ability, and personalities to accomplish the chosen goal. Their objective, in Biblical terms, is:

Train up a child in the way he should go, And when he is old he will not depart from it.
PROVERBS 22:6

This is a formidable task to say the least and surely requires honest partners of good will giving the job their best efforts. It seems to me that in comparison to building apartments, raising children is an enormously more difficult and challenging objective.

Raising children demands the utmost of cooperation between parents over a twenty-year haul. Obviously, the first step is to accept the challenge and be committed to succeed together.

The One Big Hang-Up

In my consulting room I have listened to thousands of sad stories about strains in business partnerships, friendships, marriage, and parenthood. Assuming good will, friendship, and common goals to start with, most of the strains boil down to one major issue—decision making.

What is involved in decision making? The process is the same whether it is business, friendship, or parenthood.

> *"Assuming good will, friendship, and common goals to start with, most of the strains boil down to one major issue—decision making."*

Marie and Joe

Joe and Marie are sitting in their living room. Joe is about to break some good news to his wife.

Joe: I just got a $300 per month raise. Let's invest it in a new couch.

Marie: You got a raise?! Hooray! (They melt into each other's arms and after a few friendly hugs and kisses, they resume the conversation.)

Marie: A new couch would be great, Joe. This one is looking pretty tired.

Joe: It sure is. Let's go look at some in the store.

(After some silence)

Marie: Joe…?

Joe: I'm listening. (He gives her a big hug.)

Marie: When we go to my mom's house, it's sure great to shove the dishes in a dishwasher. One of those would save me lots of work. (Pause) Let's get a dishwasher instead of a couch.

(There's a long silence.)

Marie: Joe? What are you thinking?

Joe: Why do you always contradict me? You know there's no room for a dishwasher in the kitchen. Besides, a couch will benefit the entire family, including you. Do we always have to differ over what to buy?

How do you handle a decision like this one in your home? How do you make the decision as husband and wife?

_____

_____

_____

Marie: You don't have to get mad!

Joe: I'm not mad!

Well, Joe and Marie got hung up and their conversation over his raise ended in icy silence.

The next morning breakfast was a distasteful, uncomfortable, silent ordeal. It was relief to both of them when Joe left for work.

That evening the air had cleared, supper was pleasant, and after the children were in bed, Joe and Marie had another meeting.

Joe: I'm sorry about my attitude last night.

Marie: Me too.

(They melt into each other's arms. For a moment, there is no conversation.)

Joe: I've been thinking. I thought we could price a dishwasher and a couch.

Marie: That's plenty fair enough.

They went shopping. They found out that a dishwasher would not fit in the kitchen. Couches were more expensive than they thought. The old one would do a few years. The children were small and had a tendency to jump on the couch and even accidentally spill things on it. A new couch would be more of a problem at this time than a pleasure.

> *"Sensible people will come up with reasonable decisions."*

It is strange what happens to partners. Sensible people will come up with reasonable decisions, won't they?

APPLICATION (OBEDIENCE TO GOD)

What did God teach me today:

_____

_____

Applying what God is pointing out to you is essential. How will you obey the Lord today?

_____

_____

Write a short prayer to God that summarizes your thoughts.

_____

_____

What are you going to do, say, or think today that will demonstrate obedience to God?

_____

_____

THOUGHT FOR THE DAY
Partnership in marriage is essential if good decisions are to be made.

DAY 2—DECISIONS, DECISIONS.

Remember that mysterious stranger within? You find yourself feeling, thinking, saying, and doing the strangest things.

Why?

Joe and Marie had every intention of having a happy marriage, but ended up in cool silence over a decision.

Why?

Because of the nature of people. Remember the description of people in the last chapter?

> **For the good that I will to do, I do not do; but the evil**
> **I will not to do, that I practice.**
> ROMANS 7:19

Whenever two or more people must cooperate, no matter how dedicated, cooperative, or hard working, they will sooner or later get hung up over a decision. They will come to a stalemate. Everything that could be said has been said. All the facts are in. There is nothing to be added. Still they are hung up, but they do not intend to be.

> *"Whenever two or more people must cooperate, no matter how dedicated, cooperative, or hard working, they will sooner or later get hung up over a decision."*

A Matter Of Opinion—But Whose?

Decision making reveals another side of human nature. The Bible describes it this way:

> **We have turned, every one, to his own way...**
> ISAIAH 53:6

How true. My ideas, my plans, my way of doing it sounds pretty good to me. So does yours to you. Marriage partners normally are committed to harmonious relations. Yet, sometimes your personal judgment seems better than someone else's.

The choice of a machine, of a dishwasher or a couch, is all a matter of opinion. There is no right or wrong choice. But whose opinion? The answer to this question is the key to successful partnerships.

Success in business, cooperation in marriage and parenthood—neither of these are lofty enough objectives to overcome the strong pull a person feels to go his own way, to do his own thing. "To do it my way" is the sweetest music to anyone's ears. So what do you do about this tendency? Here are some suggestions:

> *"But whose opinion? The answer to this question is the key to successful partnerships."*

1. You admit the truth about yourself ("I want my own way").

2. You confess it to the Lord.

3. You ask Him to cleanse you and to give you a spirit of cooperation.

Here is a suggested prayer—remember that prayer is talking to God—to help you make those steps:

> Dear Lord,
> I need Your help. My desire to push my own ideas drives me so hard it tends to spoil my fellowship with other people. I recognize this drive within me and I need Your help to correct it. Give me a spirit of cooperation.

What do you think would happen if you practiced these steps during your next decision making time?

_____

_____

_____

_____

Who Has the Last Word?

How do you solve the hang-ups the living room?

First is personal preparation. Each person involved in the decision needs a God-given spirit of cooperation.

Second, each person involved is committed to reaching the objectives of the partnership.

Third, someone is designated in advance to have the last word. In a business it is the president. And in parenthood it is…

It is who…?

> *"Each person involved in the decision needs a God-given spirit of cooperation."*

Who do you think should have the last word? What is your Biblical basis?

_____

_____

_____

The Most Controversial Question

The answer to that question is one of the most controversial issues of our time. Marriages break up over this issue. Let's look in once more on Joe and Marie to see how they handled this matter of decision-making.

At first their discussion about a couch or a dishwasher ended up in icy silence. The question was not settled that night. It did not need to be. Few questions require an immediate decision.

An icy silence is not the best way to end a discussion, either. But it happened. After all, we are not talking about angels. Joe and Marie are people who tend to fight for their own way, like anyone else.

This is not the first time these people got hung up over a decision. In fact they almost separated once because decisions piled up on them and the answers became a contest instead of a cooperative effort.

Fortunately, they ran into someone who introduced them to Jesus Christ. Jesus is now their Savior. They are learning to use God's Word, the Bible, to find clues on how to effectively live together. Also, they ask Jesus to help them.

APPLICATION (OBEDIENCE TO GOD)

What did God teach me today:

_____

_____

Applying what God is pointing out to you is essential. How will you obey the Lord today?

_____

_____

Write a short prayer to God that summarizes your thoughts.

_____

_____

What are you going to do, say, or think today that will demonstrate obedience to God?

_____

_____

THOUGHT FOR THE DAY
Decisions are best made when you have a Biblical foundation for making them.

DAY 3—THE CONTROVERSIAL ANSWER

They found the truth from the Bible that saved their marriage. It was the answer to the most loaded of all questions, "Who has the last word?" They found one clue when they were furious with each other over some basic issues. They both worked at the time, and these issues had stacked up:

Who makes the bed?

Who sweeps the floor?

Who washes dishes?

A red car or a blue car?

What speed do you drive on the freeway? (She said sixty; he said seventy.)

Their friend who introduced them to searching the Bible for clues, led them to what they thought was a bombshell.

The questions was: How do you solve a hang-up? The Biblical answer was:

Wives, submit to your own husbands, as to the Lord.
EPHESIANS 5:22, 23

Wowie!

When she read that, Marie hit the ceiling.

"I'm not taking orders from him," she said.

"Why not?" asked the friend.

"All he cares about is himself."

How would the wife in your family respond? Would you/she respond like this? Why?

_____

_____

_____

_____

Marie was right. Of course all she cared about was herself too. There is no way to succeed in a partnership between two people who are mad at each other and have no intention of cooperating. They had not intended to square off and oppose each other when they married, but they had not reckoned with the fact about human nature as described in Isaiah 53:6:

We have turned, every one, to his own way...

What is the iniquity of us all? My judgment must prevail.

Joe and Marie decided to try it God's way. They did not stop with just that one controversial passage. There are great truths in Ephesians 5 that are quite palatable also.

1. Do not be drunk with wine.

2. Be filled with the Spirit.

3. Have a song on your lips toward God.

4. Have a melody in your heart toward God.

5. Have a thankful spirit toward God.

6. Be subject to one another in fear of God.

7. Wives, be subject to your husbands as unto the Lord.

8. Husbands, love your wives and give yourself to them. Love them

as you would your own bodies as Christ loved the church.

Joe and Marie had the above points as their objectives. yet, their conversation about buying a couch ended up in icy silence.

What made the happy ending possible?

During the day both Joe and Marie separately realized each had drifted away from a God-given spirit of cooperation. Personal opinion had become more important than the partnership.

What do you do then? You repent, ask God to forgive and cleanse you, and return to your commitment. This made a friendly conversation possible that evening and resulted ultimately in a sensible decision about the growing problem.

Saving Marriages

When honesty and good will prevail, most decisions will be settled in a mutually agreeable fashion. When there is a stalemate, someone must have the last word.

Joe and Marie decided to try the Biblical way. God saved their marriage. When there is a stalemate, Joe settles it. Many times he depends on her judgment, especially when the children are involved.

They still drift back to their old way of fighting over a decision, but when they realize what is happening, they return to the Biblical way.

How would the wife in your family respond? Would you/she respond like this? Why?

_____

_____

_____

Our next two days will give you some tips on working together as partners. So read on tomorrow and this matter of having the last word will make more sense.

You will find being in business for yourself can be a lot of fun.

APPLICATION (OBEDIENCE TO GOD)

What did God teach me today:

_____

_____

Applying what God is pointing out to you is essential. How will you obey the Lord today?

_____

_____

Write a short prayer to God that summarizes your thoughts.

_____

_____

What are you going to do, say, or think today that will demonstrate obedience to God?

_____

_____

THOUGHT FOR THE DAY
Following Biblical instruction can change controversy into peaceful living.

DAY 4—FAMILY LEADERSHIP

Betty, age thirty-six, is speaking. "If there is one scene that I look forward to everyday, it's when my husband Bob comes home from work."

"Sometimes the kids get to him in the driveway first. Sometimes we all see him at once as he comes through the door. No matter how many times we've gone through it, his arrival always picks up the day for the rest of us."

"Maybe we've had a bad day. Maybe it's been a good day. In either case, when he pops through that door full of enthusiasm, sometimes with kids hanging all over him, I feel like saying just like they do on the talk shows:

Now...Heeeeerrrrre's Dad!"

The Prosperous Farmer

Several years ago as dean of a college, I visited a prosperous farmer whose son and daughter were students at my school. All the way to their parent's house, they spoke in the highest terms of their dad. I soon found out why.

After breakfast the first morning, I looked up and saw the father in the kitchen helping his wife with the dishes.

A little later I glanced through the window, he was out washing his son's car. During the day the daughter used her dad's car, while he used the truck. Finally, I asked him why.

"It's my way of saying a special thank you for the kids wanting to come back home. And I'm helping my wife so she has more time to spend with the kids."

> *"He was not spoiling his children. Nor was he ordered around or imposed upon."*

This pattern continued the entire weekend. The mother and father slept on cots in the basement so the guests could have the best rooms in the house and the children could use their own rooms.

This man was no slave. He was not henpecked. He did not undertake all those tasks every day, but he was willing to pitch in on special days. He was not spoiling his children. Nor was he ordered around or imposed upon.

His attitude was catching. The children helped him with the farm chores. They pitched in and helped with the housework.

Dad had set the tone. It was Jesus who said of Himself:

"For even the Son of Man did not come to be served, but to serve, and to give His life a ransom for many."
MARK 10:45

Jesus Himself, said:

...whoever desires to become great among you shall be your servant.
MARK 10:43

Give, and it will be given to you: good measure, pressed down, shaken together, and running over will be put into your bosom. For with the same measure that you use, it will be measured back to you.
LUKE 6:38

Good will makes working out the details of life simple. When good will does not exist, the activities you engage in are empty and unrewarding.

> *"Good will makes working out the details of life simple."*

Dad, Pay Attention To Us!

Ralph has this viewpoint. "When I come home I figure my work is done. I'm home. And it's up to my wife and family to make me comfortable. After all, I'm the man of the house. I work all day and deserve a rest."

Write down your thoughts concerning how you believe this kind of attitude affects the home.

_____

_____

_____

_____

Ken feels more or less the same way. His son has a habit of harassing him with an endless stream of questions as soon as he comes through the door. Ken has constructed a defense against this. He sets his son down beside him and starts reading the evening paper. His son talks on.

Ken gives out with an occasional: "Uh huh…No…Oh?…Yes…"

One evening this solid line of defense got him into trouble. On this night, he had ignored nearly all of the boy's questions, when he suddenly "came to" for one.

"What do you do all day down at your office?"

Upset over being pestered with unimportant questions, he tried to throw the boy's question aside by shooting out absentmindedly:

"Oh...nothing."

After a thoughtful pause the boy asked, "Dad, how do you know when you are through?"

What is he telling that little question machine beside him?

_____

_____

_____

Even though he has his son on the couch next to him, his mind is somewhere else. Children get the message—soon.

APPLICATION (OBEDIENCE TO GOD)

What did God teach me today:

_____

_____

60

Applying what God is pointing out to you is essential. How will you obey the Lord today?

_____

_____

Write a short prayer to God that summarizes your thoughts.

_____

_____

What are you going to do, say, or think today that will demonstrate obedience to God?

_____

_____

THOUGHT FOR THE DAY
Dad sets the tone for the whole family.

DAY 5—FAMILY PROCESSES

There are many similarities between running a business and running a family. In either organization the leader is fully responsible for the success of the organization. It is his task to see to it that plans, budgets, standards, and rules are set up. He must provide the supervision and training necessary to reach the objectives.

> "There are many similarities between running a business and running a family."

What A President Does

Permit me to share with you how this worked in my company and then make comparisons to the family. We started from scratch, and over a period of five years we built a chain of six restaurants involving 250 employees. Some of my duties as president were:

1. Set the objectives
2. Provide the finances
3. Provide buildings and equipment
4. Determine standards of quality and service
5. Set policies and rules
6. Provide standards of performance
7. Provide training and supervision

8. Provide maintenance of property and equipment
9. Provide cost controls
10. Delegate responsibility and authority

I did not do this by myself. To manage six restaurants required: (1) one general manger (2) two assistants to the general manager (3) six managers (4) twelve assistant managers (5) one office manager.

The standards, policies, procedures, and rules were not conceived by me and then handed down to the employees. They were created and changed primarily by daily interaction between the general manager and the manager.

You may wonder why it takes 22 people to manage 250 people. There are honest, cooperative, ambitious, unselfish, dependable people. Then there are dishonest, undependable, uncooperative lazy, selfish people. They come to work in a variety of moods—which affects the work. It takes that many people to maintain or restore goodwill, commitment, and cooperation. The task can be summarized best by reminding you of a Bible passage referred to in the last chapter:

Then make my joy complete by being like-minded, having the same love, being one in spirit and purpose. Do nothing out of selfish ambition or vain conceit, but in humility consider others better than yourselves.
PHILIPPIANS 2:2,3

Cooperation requires continuous, ongoing discussion, review, and change among people of goodwill. This was especially true of the relationship between my general manager and myself. What is in my mind and what I am committed to must be accepted in the general manager's mind, for he must implement my ideas with the managers and assistant managers. I need to know his mind, accept and help implement his ideas.

> *"Cooperation requires continuous, ongoing discussion, review, and change among people of goodwill."*

Look back at that verse again. Notice the two words: *like-mindedness* and *agreement*. Those are good words and attitudes that are keys to the success of any good business or family.

Setting Up the Family

How does this apply to the family? If you think of parenthood as a small business, the leaders are the husband and wife. In our day it is very likely that both work outside of the home. Still, decisions have to be made.

The family starts small. Just two people. But the family grows gradually, just like a business. The duties are as follows:

1. Set the objectives
2. Provide the finances
3. Provide food and clothing
4. Provide buildings and equipment
5. Provide maintenance of property and equipment
6. Guide the children
7. Determine standards of quality and service
8. Set policies and rules
9. Provide standards of performance
10. Provide training and supervision
11. Provide cost controls
12. Delegate responsibility and authority

See how similar this is to running a business? None of this is possible without a foundation of good will, commitment, and cooperation. To put it in Biblical terms:

Submitting to one another in the fear of God.
EPHESIANS 5:21

To put it another way, it is the job of any couple to design a harness both of them will wear. This is not the same as a husband designing a harness designed just for his wife to wear. This is a cooperative effort. Both wear the harness made of the above duties and responsibilities.

Describe the harness you would want your spouse and you to wear together. Does anything in your life need to change in order to look like the harness you just described? Explain.

_____

_____

_____

_____

_____

_____

What resources does a couple have? Time, talent, ability, and money. A family is a small business, so it requires personal involvement. There is a president and an executive vice-president. That is it. Few families can afford or want a cook, a gardener, a maid, or a business manager.

The Officers

The husband is the president. His wife may be smarter than he or may be able to get more done. She is an asset, not a liability.

In my company, for example, we had an employee who knew more about food than anyone else. He was not president of the company just because he was more knowledgeable about food. He was an employee who carried much responsibility and authority and made many decisions on his own.

> *"The husband is the president. His wife may be smarter than he or may be able to get more done, which is an asset, not a liability."*

Managing The Family

How does the husband go about managing the family? Since this book is focusing on parenthood, I will just select the topic of guiding children as an example. How does a husband fill his role of managing a family?

My wife and I were both committed to doing what was necessary to guide our children. I say *were* because our children are adults and are pursuing their own careers.

Picture the two of us having a meeting about child management. I am the president. The family is my responsibility.

My wife is the world's greatest expert on the subject of our children. She is also the executive vice-president.

We must set limits, provide supervision, and training. How does a president proceed when he has the world's greatest expert on his hands? The answer seems obvious. He leans heavily on her expertise. One would be foolish to ignore such a person. Before you would contradict or overrule this person, you had better have a good reason.

> *"How does a president proceed when he has the world's greatest expert on his hands?"*

This is exactly how we proceeded. I delegated the responsibility and authority for child guidance to my wife. Their feeding, clothing, education, social life, and duties were her responsibility. In other words, she told me how things were to be handled. This is not a cop-out on my part, it is simply drawing upon the best talent available. You may not be able to do this with your family. Work responsibilities and talents may require both to be active in these areas.

We did not have Eva's way of handling the children and Henry's way of handling the children. We had a way that both of us were committed to. We had common guidelines, policies, and limits. Eva was in charge whether I was home or not. We were of the same mind.

Even though she was in charge, there was no doubt who the president was. Yet Eva was the executive vice-president with all the authority to act as needed.

> *"Changing is not a matter of argument but of negotiation and cooperation."*

Just as in a business, policies, procedures, and limits kept changing. It required continuous on-going conversation to keep up to date. Changing is not a matter of argument but of negotiation and cooperation. It was not Eva's changing or my changing.

Rather, we change to something we are both committed to, if change is necessary. When there is good will, commitment, and cooperation under-girding an organization, hang-ups seldom occur.

Whether your work responsibilities are like Eva and mine or not, cooperation is necessary.

At our house, Eva was in charge.

United We Stand

Occasionally, one of our children would come running out to me as I came home at night and say, "Dad, can I go out tonight?"

I was in the driveway, not even in the house yet. I was in no position to answer that question. Why? The person who had been in charge of this outfit all day long was in the house and I had not consulted with her.

That woman in the house was my friend. We were on the same management team. She was the authority. What is more, she was executive vice-president of the family.

I would have been foolish to make decisions on behalf of our children without consulting her. In business, if I came to a restaurant and met the manager first, I did not give him an opinion on any big decision until I had first talked to the general manager.

Talking with my wife first was necessary before I could answer my children. I could not give them an answer when I first came home. To put it in the business vernacular, I did not have any data.

Decision making without data, may get you into trouble. That kind of decision is a guess. A husband making a decision without data will probably have to change the decision immediately.

Usually when I proposed to check with Eva, they would say, "Don't bother." They had already checked with her.

A Business Meeting At Home

I had many meetings with the key person in my business. We sat down together to plan what is best for the future and evaluated what we had been doing in the past. We made some changes. We might even revise what we had been doing up to then.

The home should be the same. Marriage partners sit down and review the day, the week, or the interim during the time the husband has been away—or while the wife has been away.

You do not need to ask if there have been any problems while one of you has been gone. There will be problems. The two basic questions are:

1. What problems did you have you were able to solve?
2. What problems did you have your were unable to solve?

Start from there. Maybe you will make some changes. The two of you may evaluate the rules again. Whatever, the job is to chart the course for your family.

Not two courses. One. Not one way when Dad is home and another way when Mom is home. I have heard children say, "I can get along O.K. with my dad when he is home and Mom is gone." Or, "I can get along all right with my mother when she is home and Father is gone, but when they are together it is difficult because my parents do not agree."

Agreement and unity comprise the foundation on which you build an effective family life.

If you and your wife function as president and executive vice-president, you will discover that being in business for yourself—the family business can be a lot of fun.

Note the word "if." If there is goodwill, commitment, and cooperation. Remember, we are talking about people, not angels. There were times when ill will, selfishness, stubbornness, and anger would more accurately describe one or both of us. Neither of us would repent. Such a spirit between us could last days or weeks. Problem solving will cease happening as long as such a condition exists.

Parenting will expose the soul. Each person must face the presence of that mysterious stranger—sin. Negotiation must be tabled. The only way to deal with sin is to look to God. No human being can help. Repentance before God leading to forgiveness, cleansing, and yielding to the Holy Spirit's control is the only way to restore goodwill between spouses. Then you can proceed with problem solving.

APPLICATION (OBEDIENCE TO GOD)

What did God teach me today:

_____

_____

Applying what God is pointing out to you is essential. How will you obey the Lord today?

_____

_____

Write a short prayer to God that summarizes your thoughts.

_____

_____

What are you going to do, say, or think today that will demonstrate obedience to God?

_____

_____

THOUGHT FOR THE DAY
Agreement and unity comprise a foundation
on which you build an effective family life.

UNIT 5

MOM—MRS. EXECUTIVE VICE-PRESIDENT

THOUGHT STARTER

A husband without a wife is not the most effective organization.

MEMORY VERSE

Who can find a virtuous wife? For her worth is far above rubies.

PROVERBS 31:10

DAY 1—SOME KIND OF WOMAN!

Proverbs 31 is an incredible chapter. Rather, it contains an incredible list of characteristics, roles, and responsibilities. Can you believe they are all found in the same woman?

Here is that list:

Seamstress extraordinary, small businesswoman, purchaser of goods, obtainer of food, time and schedule organizer, real estate purchaser, physical fitness expert, teacher, ambitious, fears the Lord, clothes purchaser, community worker, good citizen, social worker, dietitian, good dresser, saleswoman, tireless, lets her job speak for itself, praised by family and community alike. That is some kind of woman! Hardly someone who just keeps house.

Is it not a pity we so often ignore the Bible? The roles and characteristics of the woman described in this chapter could serve as an outline for any woman's awareness course.

Yet modern day literature would have us believe that the tremendous talent and ability residing in women is a recent discovery.

Any man who has not taken note of the fact that women are on par with men as intelligent, creative people just has not been paying attention.

> *"Any man who hasn't taken note of the fact that women are on a par with men as intelligent, creative people just hasn't been paying attention."*

A Good Lesson

During my junior high school days, the local

newspaper had a young writers' club. Our English teacher required all of us to write a weekly story for the club. She would pick the best story and send it to the paper for publication.

Nine out of ten weeks, the best story was written by one of the girls.

Also, during those days I was given charge of managing school-wide candy sales to raise money for our extracurricular activities.

The two top "salesmen" were always girls.

I had another responsibility during my high school days that showed me something about women. I was assigned to be in charge of the mimeographing at the school. I started recruiting workers…some boys and some girls.

Of the two groups, I soon found that the girls proved more efficient, trustworthy, and cooperative than the boys.

In college, the top student in my class was a girl. No matter what the rest of us did, she was always out there in front of us. Even so, being top student in the class was not enough for her. She also was president of several leading clubs at the school.

As I made my way through the educational, business, and church worlds, I noticed that a woman can direct a Vacation Bible School just as well, if not better, than a man. In my business, the person we assigned to be in charge of the money was a woman.

Why do you suppose women are so effective?

_____

_____

_____

I never cease to marvel at the skill and ease with which my wife can produce a delicious meal. The finest chef may match her skill, but I doubt if anyone could exceed her. To her, cooking is fun.

People often visit us for the express purpose of seeing me. They might spend eight hours with me and only half an hour with my wife (at a meal).

Even though I helped them, it seems that whenever they write back, what they remember most is my wife and her cooking—not me. Her outlook toward cooking shows.

It is also remarkable how quickly she can breeze through the house to straighten it up. She also takes care of our travel arrangements as competently as the finest travel agent.

The Constant Complaint

On the other hand, Janie, age forty-four, wails:

> There must be more meaning to life than this! In the morning, Dad and the kids all descend upon the kitchen, where I feed them breakfast.

At noon, part of that original crew returns to have their stomachs filled again.

Then they all disappear and I don't see them again until early evening when they suddenly materialize just in time to have their tummies filled again. Why, all our kitchen is…is a filling station! And I'm the attendant.

Mary Ann, age twenty-eight, echoes the sentiments:

All through high school, my parents saved money for my college. I worked after school and during summers. Then, together we struggled to pay my way through college. Finally, I received my degree.

Then, after I completed college, instead of using that degree, I got married. Now, I change diapers, sweep the floors, cook meals, and wash dishes all day. Did I need a college degree for that? I've never felt so worthless in all my life.

There is a lot of difference between grinding out breakfast like a station attendant and providing nutritious meals and fun for the family and their guests.

Janie and Mary Ann ought to sit down and talk with their husbands and solve a real problem in their family management.

APPLICATION (OBEDIENCE TO GOD)
What did God teach me today:

_____

_____

Applying what God is pointing out to you is essential. How will you obey the Lord today?

_____

_____

Write a short prayer to God that summarizes your thoughts.

_____

_____

What are you going to do, say, or think today that will demonstrate obedience to God?

_____

_____

THOUGHT FOR THE DAY
A good wife is far more precious than jewels.

DAY 2—WEARISOME OR WONDROUS?

Details can be wearisome, can't they? Have you ever thought of how many ear holes and nose holes a doctor examines each day? Does he think of his job in terms of nose holes or in terms of healing people?

Ralph, who works in a kitchen cabinet shop, sees himself as a craftsman of wooden works of art. Another employee in the same shop has a different outlook. He is a grumpy, crabby, griper who only saws boards, inhales sawdust, and gets glue all over his fingers. Both do the same job. Both make beautiful cabinets.

What about the soggy mouths a dentist looks into during his working hours? Does he look at it as a job examining soggy mouths or a job of helping people to good dental health?

Mr. Everything

Let's take a look at a unique situation: Valerie has a business of her own. Her husband, Erik, stays at home and does the housework. He sees the children off to school each day. He helps with the shopping and the cooking, but this still leaves lots of time on his hands.

Erik has become a volunteer worker at church and a busy one. He is perfectly happy and loves his role.

To meet Erik, you would think you had met the ideal man. Big. Handsome. Personable.

But he is a loafer.

He once had a responsible job. Then came a demotion, and then another. Finally, he was fired—for laziness.

So Valerie, a competent, responsible person, stepped into the gap. She got a job, and then started her own business. For ten years, she has supported the family.

Valerie's situation is exactly what many wives desire. She is free from the routines of managing a home.

But all is not well. She prefers to be a homemaker.

> *"It's not fair, Dr. Brandt," says she. "I want to be home doing housework and taking care of the kids. Erik won't let me."*

"It's not fair, Dr. Brandt," says she. "I want to be home doing housework and taking care of the kids. Erik won't let me."

What advice would you give this couple?

_____

_____

_____

There it is. According to my years of observation in the consulting room the basic cause of marital discord is conflict and ill will between couples.

The routines must be handled, no doubt about that. The debate is over, "who does what."

For Erik and Valerie, it is a standoff. It has been a ten-year debate. No one has the last word, so the issue can not be settled.

Any woman or man needs to be effectively and happily busy. However, contentment does not come by dropping one set of routines for another. Erik and Valerie found that out.

The division of responsibilities between a husband and wife is, of course, negotiable. A couple can only come to mutually agreeable decisions as both parties are committed to the mutual interests of one another and a final authority is established.

The Swimming Instructor

Sarah was not effectively busy. She had four children ages 2 through 14 and a husband who was in business for himself.

"I don't have any big trouble with the children. I host the parties for Edgar when he's entertaining. I take care of the house. I help out in the business. Still, I've got a lot of time on my hands that I don't want to spend vegetating in front of *The Edge of Night*.

So she and her husband decided that she should volunteer to teach a swimming class at the YMCA. It was not that she hated housework or managing children. She had time on her hands and a busy mind.

Her husband wholeheartedly encouraged Sarah. The baby sitting service at the YMCA enabled her to take the baby with her to her class.

Sarah was good—so good, that within a year she was teaching four courses at the YMCA. Even though she was now spending a total of about ten hours on four different days at the Y, she still easily managed to meet her primary responsibilities as mother and wife.

Sarah could have become bored. But, while balancing her primary goals beautifully, she went out and became effectively busy. Not every wife and mother needs "extra" things to do. Each husband and wife must make a decision as to what is right for their family.

Have you become bored in the details? If so, describe your feelings then propose a solution.

_____

_____

_____

The Girl Who Was Tops In Her Class

The same was true of Linda. A very creative person, she had graduated from college at the top of her class and then immediately married.

She eventually had two children, but she was becoming bored. She suggested to her husband they start a children's program for their small church, which had trouble recruiting leaders.

"But I want to do a good job," she said when she suggested it to him.

"I'm all for it. Let's go," he replied.

Together, they threw themselves into the task and came up with a unique program for the children ages 3-12 of their church.

Drawing on her training, she helped plan the weekly schedule. She contacted speakers, picked up films and film strips. She did artwork, set up puppet ideas, and started a Christian book reading program.

The program helped turn the entire trend of the church around. The church had been losing families who had elementary age children. Now, they stayed. The church grew. Others heard about the program and wanted to know more.

The church was so delighted that on Linda's birthday they sent her a beautiful bouquet of flowers with the signature, "Happy birthday! From the parents of Grace Church."

Also, the two of them decided Linda was the better storyteller of the team. So she has been telling a series of stories for the weekly gatherings. She is now working on the project of making some of the stories into books.

"And it would not have happened if Linda and her husband had not realized she wasn't effectively busy."

It would not have happened if Linda and her husband had not realized she was not effectively busy.

APPLICATION (OBEDIENCE TO GOD)

What did God teach me today:

_____

_____

Applying what God is pointing out to you is essential. How will you obey the Lord today?

_____

_____

Write a short prayer to God that summarizes your thoughts.

_____

_____

What are you going to do, say, or think today that will demonstrate obedience to God?

_____

_____

THOUGHT FOR THE DAY
Details are boring if you do not see purpose or become "effectively busy."

DAY 3 — HAPPINESS REQUIRES TEAMWORK!

Then, there's Margie. She is a bitter, resentful woman who constantly gripes about her home and her husband. She, too, is a volunteer worker...with the Red Cross. She is a driver.

If a person needs to go downtown to get a welfare check, or someone gives blood and then passes out, or an elderly person needs to go to the hospital for vital shots—Margie drives them.

Margie does not enjoy it one minute. She gripes about the "miserable people." She gripes just as much as she does about her home and husband.

Two volunteers—Linda and Margie. Why are they so different? They have two different problems. Linda needs to be effectively busy. Margie needs to experience a new relationship with Jesus Christ.

Busyness does not take care of your spirit. You must make a distinction between dealing with your spirit and dealing with the untapped use of your talent and intelligence.

> *"Busyness does not take care of your spirit."*

If you are not "effectively busy" what does that tell you about your spirit?

_____

_____

_____

_____

Two Professors

When I was going to college, I met a professor who was the main influence on my views of parenthood. Her name was Ethel Waring, and she was an incredible person.

She was happy. She was radiant. She was an inspiring college professor. What made her that way? Simple. She was a happy woman.

I know another woman college professor. Her reason for teaching is not so she will be effectively busy. She is teaching to get away from her husband, whom she hates.

> *"Her college teaching hasn't made a happy woman out of her, because it is an escape from another situation that she refuses to solve."*

Her college teaching has not made a happy woman out of her, because it is an escape from another situation that she refuses to solve.

Her busyness has made her even more unhappy, for she keeps comparing her husband (who is really a nice, competent guy) with some of the other male professors. She goes home and often takes potshots at her husband.

What is she doing? She is multiplying her misery by not only being a hateful woman toward her husband but also being a phony at work.

Good-Bye To Scrambled Eggs

Statistics tell a story, too. More than any time in history, women who can not face the scrambled eggs in the morning are becoming working mothers.

More than sixty percent of all women with children age 6 to 17 worked last year. The number one reason given was economic necessity. Right behind that reason, however was boredom. It is obvious there is widespread discontentment among women and men.

> *"More than sixty percent of all women with children age 6 to 17 worked last year."*

But the fruit of the Spirit is love, joy peace, longsuffering, kindness, goodness, faithfulness, gentleness, self-control.
Against such there is no law.
GALATIANS 5:22, 23

Competence and intelligence...organizational ability. These are characteristics of both men and women. They need to be expressed.

This expression does not change the spirit, whether a man or a woman. There are men who are wasting their talents, too.

Meet The Veep

In most businesses, the two top officers are the president and the executive vice-president. The president oversees the company and helps set the main plan and policies for the company. He may travel many different places to represent the company.

When it comes to the day in and day out running of the business, the executive vice-president is usually the key officer. The executive vice-president really makes things run.

While the president may be responsible for many final decisions, he rarely makes a decision without leaning heavily on the advice of someone in the company, usually the executive VP, who is a very knowledgeable, authoritative person in his own right. These individuals are friends and sense a high degree of accomplishment as they work together. It is difficult to distinguish one's input from the other.

This is a perfect description of the roles of a father and a mother. While dad might be known as the head of the home and responsible for many of the ultimate decisions, he does not run the family on a day in and day out basis. The mother does that. She is the executive vice-president.

> *"If she does her homework, she is the most knowledgeable, best informed person in the organization."*

If she does her homework, she is the most knowledgeable, best informed person in the organization. As the years go by and she grows in her knowledge of the children, her input becomes increasingly valuable. As her recommendations are put into practice, the resulting success makes her an increasingly valuable person in the organization. Her influence is enormous and her wisdom is one of the most important assets of the organization.

Such an authoritative person (an expert) makes decisions as necessary within the policies of the organization without consulting anyone. Managing the family is a responsibility many women can handle easily with much time to spare.

Expanding Mom's Role

Some mothers could not possibly take on any additional family responsibilities. Then, there are those moms who breeze through the chores at home and are ready for something else by 10 o'clock every morning. My wife is that way.

When my wife and I first started in this business of raising a family, we got together and listed all of our responsibilities. (Notice I said our responsibilities, not my wife's responsibilities or my responsibilities.)

Just a few of the many we detailed were: housecleaning, money management, cooking, writing, radio work, children, cleaning the yard, travel agent, running a business, raising money, and food purchasing.

Then we divvied them up—she handled the money management, travel agent, housecleaning, cooking, children, food purchasing, and a bunch more. I was assigned writing, radio work, cleaning the yard, running a business, and raising money. These were assignments on the basis of training, ability, interest, and necessity.

How we met the responsibilities was not the question. The assignment was simple. These were the responsibilities each of us was to carry out.

If my wife decided to add responsibilities outside the home...fine. But she would have to figure out some way to carry out her primary tasks.

Take a look at your family. Have you listed responsibilities for one another. If not, do so now. Are you carrying out your primary responsibility?

> *"How we met the responsibilities was not the question. The assignment was simple: these were the responsibilities each of us was to carry out."*

_____

_____

_____

The same went for any other activities I took on. It was fine as long as I kept the primary activities going. Of course, they kept changing as the children grew and demands on our time changed.

In all our planning and assigning, we kept one thing in mind—our plans must be a family plans. We made sure to remember that it was a Brandt plan, no Henry's plan or Eva's plan. It was our plan, and we had to carry out our responsibilities.

If you are not effectively busy at home, the next time you have one of those business meetings between husband and wife, well, volunteer for some more work! It sure beats being bored.

APPLICATION (OBEDIENCE TO GOD)
What did God teach me today:

_____

_____

Applying what God is pointing out to you is essential. How will you obey the Lord today?

_____

_____

Write a short prayer to God that summarizes your thoughts.

_____

_____

What are you going to do, say, or think today that will demonstrate obedience to God?

_____

_____

> ## THOUGHT FOR THE DAY
> ### Busyness does not take care of your spirit,
> ### God does!

DAY 4—DECISIONS REQUIRE TEAMWORK

Many decisions can and should be made without involving the president of a company or the husband in a family.

A meeting is being held in a business. Present are the general manager (number two person in the organization), two assistants, and six managers. The question under discussion: a letdown in five of the restaurants on uniform cleanliness and crispness.

"I'll admit it," says one of the managers. "We have let down on this, but only because of the policy."

"Right," says another manager. "If we follow the policy and send an employee home every time he reports to work with a uniform that isn't neat, then he gets mad and threatens to quit."

"And business is booming so much, that if we are short even one waiter or waitress because of such a policy it really cuts into our ability to give the people good service."

"No good service...no good business," adds another.

"I disagree," exclaims one of the assistants. "We've always held to a standard of cleanliness, right?"

Everyone agrees.

"Well, if we start allowing our uniforms to get sloppy, the entire operation begins to get sloppy. Let down a standard here and then a standard there. Pretty soon, we're sloppy all around. And then we'll really lose customers."

The debate is now on. And after a little more discussion, it is obvious the group is hopelessly split. It is time for the general manager to make a decision. The neat uniform policy will stand. Everyone accepts it and that is that.

After the meeting is over, the general manager calls me and gives me a verbal report. The decision is over. The authority for the general manager to operate this way comes from the president. Operating on this basis is decided on the general manager's record of performance. He has first hand contact with the managers and on the basis of his performance has demonstrated his competence.

"I've Made Some Changes Around Here!"

A family organization is much smaller than a restaurant chain, of course. There is a president and executive vice-president, or man and wife.

Joe and Marie are sitting at the kitchen table. Two boys, ages eight and ten, are playing outside.

Marie: I made some changes around here.

Joe: What are they?

Marie: I've pushed bedtime up a half hour and also the kids must take their shoes off on the landing.

Joe: O.K.

That night, Joe puts the children to bed. This was Marie's job, but she was too tired and asked him to do it. Each boy griped to dad because he had to take his shoes off on the landing. His response to them was:

"That's the way it is."

Go, Team, Go!

The authority for Marie to operate this way comes from Joe. It is based on her record. She has firsthand contact on a daily basis with the children and on the basis of her performance has demonstrated her competence.

How do you and your spouse discuss rules before making decisions?

_____

_____

_____

_____

Guiding children is the responsibility of the organization. Joe and Marie are a team. They work together. They care about each other. Of course he will put the children to bed if she is tired. In their style of life, he may put them to bed often. The pattern of responsibilities is a negotiable matter. There is no competition here, just cooperation.

What else does Marie do besides keep house and manage the children? Whatever she and Joe agree is reasonable.

What else does Joe do besides his income producing job? Whatever he and Marie agree is reasonable.

Agreement is the key word. It is a team effort. Unresolved conflicts are the soil for weak marriages.

> "Agreement is the key word. It is a team effort. Unresolved conflicts are the soil for weak marriages."

Nancy Wanted a Washing Machine...

Nancy and Kevin could not agree on who should control the money, as well as other conflicts of opinion. There were many verbal barrages. She wanted a washer and dryer. He said she would get them only over his dead body. Her response was to buy them.

In retaliation, Kevin went on a drinking spree that lasted several days. For spite, he bought a new station wagon. Nancy did not enjoy her appliances. They were a rebuke to her every time she used them. Nor did her husband enjoy driving that new station wagon.

Here were two people who had acquired some equipment that should have given them joy and satisfaction. Instead, these useful things became a continuing bone of contention. Behind the strife over money was the unsettled question of submission. Both persons were asserting a spirit of independence and selfishness. They were hardly a team.

APPLICATION (OBEDIENCE TO GOD)

What did God teach me today:

_____

_____

Applying what God is pointing out to you is essential. How will you obey the Lord today?

_____

_____

Write a short prayer to God that summarizes your thoughts.

_____

_____

What are you going to do, say, or think today that will demonstrate obedience to God?

_____

_____

THOUGHT FOR THE DAY
Submission requires teamwork.

DAY 5 — TWO VOICES — ONE TUNE

Once my daughter came to me and said, "The church youth group is going roller skating. Mom said I can't go. Can I go?"

I was not in a position to make that decision. I did not know if my wife had said that. So I simply checked with my wife, who replied, "Well, the condition for going roller skating was that she have her homework done."

"That's right," I added, "we agreed on that."

"Well, she doesn't have it done."

That was simple; case dismissed. However, this is what happened in another family. Carole had asked her mother if she might go roller skating with the church group and Mom replied, "No, you were at prayer meeting last night, and you studied late the night before."

"Ah, let her go," Dad cut in. "She's only young once."

"But Carole needs her rest," Mom insisted. Then the seesaw argument began, and both mother and father were soon angry.

The incident was a common one in Carole's life. As a result her head and heart spun with confusion and revolt so much that she eventually came to me for help.

This is deadly. Frequently the husband has one plan and wife another. When the husband goes away to work, the wife says to herself, "Finally...he's gone! Now we can get back to normal around here."

It is so important that parents speak with two voices but only one tune. Joe and Marie decided to work that way.

> *"It is so important that parents speak with two voices but only one tune."*

Do you and your spouse speak with two voices but one tune to the children? How do you know that you do?

_____

_____

_____

_____

Call Of The Beauty Shop

Joe and Marie agreed to go camping. But finding a time proved difficult. Joe wanted to go this weekend, but Marie had a beauty shop appointment Saturday afternoon. After some discussion about canceling, Joe realized it would be an unnecessary nuisance for her. He could not go the following week, so they planned camping in three weeks. This is no big deal among friends who really care about each other.

When they did go, they were all together on the project. At the camp site, Marie became acquainted with the lady in the tent next door. Marie was enjoying frying hamburgers beside the lake. Her neighbor was griping about being dragged away from home to endure the nuisance of outdoor cooking.

They were in the same spot with similar equipment, both cooking beside a lake. The difference was in the spirit of the women and their relationships with their husbands.

Now...The Children

We are through talking about the man now. And we are through talking about the woman. We are assuming a contented man and a contented woman. So let's get on with the job of parenthood.

Each family should have as its goal:

Train up a child in the way he should go, And when he is old
he will not depart from it.

PROVERBS 22:6

This is not a woman's job—nor a man's. It is the task of the partnership.

> *"This is not a woman's job—nor a man's. It is the task of the partnership."*

Assuming good will, friendship, and commitment, two highly competent people will get on with the job.

If you were to sum up the content of the last chapter and this chapter in one word, that word would be "submission." Assuming good will, we mean a man and a woman submitting to a mutually acceptable and agreeable plan for guiding the affairs of the family. It is like wearing a two part harness.

Do you and your spouse have a mutually acceptable and agreed plan for guiding the affairs of your family? Explain.

_____

_____

_____

When a decision is to be made, and the facts involved lead a couple to a stalemate, the husband will settle it—after careful consideration of his wife's recommendations. He should have some very good reasons if he overrules her judgment. Put into Biblical terms:

Submitting to one another in the fear of God. Wives, submit to your own
husbands, as to the Lord. For the husband is head of the wife, as also Christ
is head of the church; and He is the Savior of the body. Therefore, just as the
church is subject to Christ, so let the wives be to their own husbands in
everything. Husbands, love your wives, just as Christ also loved the church
and gave Himself for it, that He might sanctify and cleanse it with the
washing of water by the word, that He might present it to Himself a
glorious church, not having spot or wrinkle or any such thing, but that
it should be holy and without blemish. So husbands ought to love
own wives as their own bodies; he who loves his wife loves himself.

EPHESIANS 5:21-28

What a partnership must do to guide the children is the subject of the rest of this book.

APPLICATION (OBEDIENCE TO GOD)

What did God teach me today:

_____

_____

Applying what God is pointing out to you is essential. How will you obey the Lord today?

_____

_____

Write a short prayer to God that summarizes your thoughts.

_____

_____

What are you going to do, say, or think today that will demonstrate obedience to God?

_____

_____

THOUGHT FOR THE DAY
A contented man and a contented woman are needed for the job of parenthood.

UNIT 6

THE FOUNDATION FOR

DISCIPLINE—LOVE AND

CONVICTION

THOUGHT STARTER

All forms of discipline should be used on the foundation of love.

MEMORY VERSE

Love suffers long and is kind; love does not envy;...bears all things, believes all things, hopes all things, endures all things.
1 CORINTHIANS 13:4, 7

DAY 1—CAN I LOVE MY CHILD TOO MUCH?

God's word instructs us to love one another earnestly from the heart (1 Peter 1:22). If this verse applies at all, it surely applies to parents in their relations with their children. Parents will surely want to give their children tender, loving, sacrificial care.

> *"Parents will surely want to give their children tender, loving, sacrificial care."*

The Biblical standard of love is described in 1 Corinthians 13:4-8. It has nine components:

patience	kindness
generosity	humility
courtesy	unselfishness
good temper	purity of heart
sincerity	

Such love is a matter of the Spirit, not something that you do or withdraw. It is obvious that hugs and kisses, or generous deeds without a loving spirit behind them are simply empty motions. As one man put it, "I kiss my wife good-bye, but her lips are hard." This couple steadfastly keeps up the motions of expressing affection, but the Spirit is missing.

The same holds true in dealing with children. Love is not something you do; it is something within you. Your love ought to be constant, not related to your child's behavior. In love you help your child to repeat acceptable behavior and in love you restrain him, if necessary, from repeating unacceptable behavior.

> *"Your love ought to be constant, not related to your child's behavior."*

The episode of Terry and the nursery school teacher shows us the value of love as the foundation in training children. Terry wanted a tricycle that another boy was using. The teachers had been making good progress with Terry in overcoming the habit of biting other children who resisted him. He had not bitten anyone for a long time.

> *"Their reactions did not depend on the conduct of the children, but on their own spirit."*

This day Terry came in sleepy and crabby. He wanted a tricycle that a playmate was using. The playmate refused to give it up, so Terry bit him. The child screamed and as the teachers approached the scene both children were in tears.

How would the teachers react? Would they be angry, disgusted, furious? Or would they be kindly, tender, compassionate? Their reactions did not depend on the conduct of the children, but on their own spirit.

In this case, both teachers were kind, tender, and compassionate. One drew the bitten child aside to comfort and find out what happened. The other teacher drew Terry into a corner to find out from him what had happened and to comfort him. "I forgot," was Terry's explanation. The teacher reminded him that biting would not be tolerated and that he must remain out of the play area until he could play happily. She made a mental note to watch him more closely the rest of the day.

A few minutes later Terry walked up to the teacher and said, "Will you help me get a tricycle, please?" The teacher's approach to Terry would have been wrong if she had become furious, glaring at the child, and shouting, "Didn't we tell you you can't bite anyone?" She would also be wrong to blame him for her own attitude.

Love does not mean inaction or letting children run wild. Let me emphasize that. When a child misbehaves, something must be done. You can and should deal with your child's most obnoxious conduct in a gentle but firm way. There is a difference between gentle firmness, and hostile firmness. A basic foundation of love and

> *There is a difference between gentle firmness, and hostile firmness.*

tenderness for the child, no matter what the behavior at the moment, is an important invisible tool in training children. Your spirit makes the difference. You know the difference—and so does your child.

When, in a spirit of hostility and anger, you strike at your child, you fail to help him and you hurt yourself. This striking need not be just physical. Sharp words or a stinging silence can be just as painful to the child as violently administered physical punishment.

Can you remember a time when you disciplined in hostility? How did you feel afterwards? What did you do about it?

_____

_____

_____

_____

Admittedly none of us can claim perfection. What then shall we do when a hostile spirit grips us? Repent, and seek God's forgiveness and his grace and patience.

The apostle Peter points out the need for an attitude of affection. He urges us in these words:

Since you have purified your souls in obeying the truth through the Spirit in sincere love of the brethren, love one another fervently with a pure heart.
1 PETER 1:22

The understanding that many people have of the place of love in guiding their children is reflected in such questions as:

"Should I withdraw my love when I punish my child?"

"Should I show that I love him after I punish him?"

When parents ask, "Should I withdraw affection from my child in order to keep him in line?"—the case of Mrs. Jamesy answers that question. After her daughter Carole had run away several times she brought her to me to see if I could help.

Carole considered her mother a cruel person. Her mother slapped Carole or pulled her hair if she dallied at the dishes or her homework. For as long as Carole could remember, her mother had threatened or punished her to try to make her behave and follow orders.

In bitterness Carole did everything opposite to her mother's directions. Though a Christian, she deliberately disobeyed her mother.

Mrs. Jamesy truly wanted to be a good mother, but she thought that it was harmful to be friendly or affectionate toward Carole when Carole misbehaved. So she would hardly turn to God for love when she considered love on such an occasion was "bad."

I had to help Mrs. Jamesy see that Carole had grounds for doubt that her mother loved her. Harshness and conflict produced unhappy scenes that overshadowed their relationship. Mrs. Jamesy realized for the first time why Carole rebelled so easily.

She saw also that returning bitterness for bitterness fed the rebellion in her daughter's heart.

I assured her it was all right to feel friendly toward a rebel child and still keep high standards. The home atmosphere changed from one of tenseness to love and understanding. Carole softened. Both now appreciate a God-directed love that binds them together.

How much bad behavior should you go along with before withdrawing your love? How much stubbornness will justify your burst of anger? Where is the line? There is no line. If your love breaks down, you need to repent.

It is said of God that He chastens whom He loves. It is also written:

> **Now no chastening seems to be joyful for the present, but grievous; nevertheless, afterward it yields the peaceable fruit of righteousness to those who have been trained by it.**
> HEBREWS 12:11

APPLICATION (OBEDIENCE TO GOD)

What did God teach me today:

_____

_____

Applying what God is pointing out to you is essential. How will you obey the Lord today?

_____

_____

Write a short prayer to God that summarizes your thoughts.

_____

_____

What are you going to do, say, or think today that will demonstrate obedience to God?

_____

_____

THOUGHT FOR THE DAY
Love for your child should be constant,
not related to your child's behavior.

DAY 2—A LOVING SPIRIT

Obviously, chastening, or correcting, is not a happy experience for the child, but in love you look beyond the present. Your task is not to keep your child smiling today at any price; it is to help him become a mature, responsible person by dealing with the situation at hand in a loving spirit.

Praise for a job well done reassures a child. Admonition for a job poorly done lets him know he is not learning well. Neither praise nor admonition is necessarily evidence of love or the lack of love. As an example, you can praise someone for having performed a beautiful solo and at the same time be filled with jealousy or animosity toward the person. You can admonish a child for doing a poor job of cleaning his room in a kindly spirit.

Can you correct your child with love? Affectionately? If not, you ought not deal with him until you can. The following incident illustrates disciplinary action where the mother's spirit needed correction.

One morning a mother of three children walked into the kitchen humming happily to herself. Her three boys were grouped around the kitchen sink chattering happily. She thought, "My, they're getting along nicely together." Then to her dismay she saw what they were doing. On the counter were piled a dozen eggshells and a bowl of the raw eggs.

The mother was enraged and proceeded to give the boys an angry lecture, telling them that for the rest of the day each must stay in the house and be isolated. This is what the boys were doing: One had gotten the idea that he would poke a hole in the end of a raw egg, empty it out, and as a joke throw it at his mother. Emptying the contents of the egg proved to be a very interesting experience, so they did it to another egg. They enjoyed it so much that they went through a dozen eggs.

After her angry tirade, the mother began to think more rationally. Here she was enraged, spoiling her day for herself and for her children over a dollar's worth of eggs. She was ashamed, repented, called her children and acknowledged that she had acted in a very inappropriate way toward the incident. Then she made it plain that their little deed nevertheless was not to be repeated again. Permission to do such things was needed from her. Everyone was relieved. That noon they all enjoyed the scrambled eggs and later that day they had scrambled egg snacks.

For another example of discipline based on a lack of love, look at the case of Mrs. Gordons.

"I love Betty very much and she knows it. But why is she so rebellious? In coming to you, I thought you might help," Mrs. Gordons told me.

This mother was a sincere Christian, and her teenage daughter had been a continual object of her prayers. She could not get Betty to study, do daily chores properly, get along with her brother, or even eat properly. It was a mother-daughter battle, and it distressed Mrs. Gordons terribly. "It's been very trying, believe me," she said.

Probing for the cause of the festering trouble, I asked what her feelings were when Betty defied her.

She confessed her impatience, anger, and resentment. "But in spite of that," she hastened to add, "I love my daughter very much. Don't you think I've proved this by the torture I've been through in keeping to myself the irritation she causes me?"

It shocked Mrs. Gordons when I said, "Your bitter feelings toward Betty are not feelings of love."

"How can you say such a thing?" she cried.

I opened my Bible to 1 Corinthians 13 and pointed out God's description of love. Love is kind...longsuffering. Kindness and longsuffering are fruit of the Holy Spirit produced within the surrendered Christian.

> "Hiding your impatience and resentment does not alter the fact that these are present in your heart."

"Hiding your impatience and resentment does not alter the fact that these are present in your heart," I told her. "These are not the ingredients of love. These are products of your selfish nature. You may pretend to Betty—and to yourself—that they do not exist, but they do!"

Mrs. Gordons was very surprised when I traced her heart anguish to her efforts to act loving rather than to be loving.

"Do you mean that Betty should be allowed to get away with what she does?" she demanded.

"Not at all," I answered. "Your daughter's behavior must be dealt with. Before you can deal with it effectively though, you must deal with your own inner spirit."

Months later Mrs. Gordons understood that if she were truly to love Betty, the impatience and resentment would have to be replaced by genuine patience, kindness, and gentleness. "I'm not capable of patience," she said desperately one day. "It is so hard to be kind."

She was right. Patience needed to be added. It comes from God. He will give it to her when she sees that she lacks it and asks God for it.

She finally dropped her defense and asked God to give her the love she lacked. She discovered God gives the measure of overflowing love He is asked to give, and she could deal with Betty in love, whether or not her daughter responded. Is it not strange that people work hard at acting lovingly, and resist the fact that they can be loving in spirit?

Betty did respond, however, and their home is now the happy Christian one it should be!

Who sets the tone in a family? The parents or the children? We often hear parents complain, "I get so tired of kids! They wear me out." Mothers of preschoolers have said to me, "If my three-year-old would behave, I'd be happy." These women were serious. Imagine how unhappy adults would be if their happiness depended on the behavior of preschoolers—or children of any age! The fellowship between you and your child may be broken but it need not be broken on your part. For example, God will not let you do as you please and give you peace of mind at the same time. He allows you to suffer when you do wrong, but He is ever ready to accept you when you turn back. He appeals to you constantly.

"Come to Me, all you who labor and are heavy laden, and I will give you rest."
MATTHEW 11:28

God has not broken fellowship with you, you have cut yourself off from Him. He would do you a disservice if He let you have your evil way with no consequences, even as you would hurt your child by letting him have his evil way with no consequences. When you are ready to confess your sins, God is waiting to hear you.

What is your home like? Is it warm and friendly or cold and hostile? Explain what your home is like.

_____

_____

_____

_____

_____

A warm, friendly home is a matter of the Spirit. Home management comes in many styles. Some home management styles are strict, and some are lenient. The style does not make the difference, the Spirit does.

> *A warm, friendly home is a matter of the Spirit."*

Every family faces the same basic challenges. Among family members are differences in age, personality, interest, needs, and capacities. We all know families who manage to operate smoothly. In love, the parents make it their business to be sensitive to the needs of each member and meet them without injuring any other member.

APPLICATION (OBEDIENCE TO GOD)

What did God teach me today:

_____

_____

Applying what God is pointing out to you is essential. How will you obey the Lord today?

_____

_____

Write a short prayer to God that summarizes your thoughts.

_____

_____

What are you going to do, say, or think today that will demonstrate obedience to God?

_____

_____

THOUGHT FOR THE DAY
A warm, friendly home is a matter of the Spirit.

DAY 3 —ADULT CONVICTION-CONFIDENT EXPECTATION

This is a non-Biblical sounding term that every parent must understand.

By *confident expectation* I mean that you are doing or requiring something you believe is in the best interests of the child. If you are you will have enough conviction to see it through.

There are two assumptions in addition:

1. The parent's manner is friendly, gentile, and firm.
2. Your partner is in agreement with you.

In Biblical terminology, one of the ten commandments says it best:

"Honor your father and your mother, that your days may be long upon the land which the Lord your God is giving you."
EXODUS 20:12

This verse implies certain conditions:

1. Any parent reading that verse must understand that it means to honor your children's grandpa and grandma.
2. It implies that you and your partner honor one another.
3. It implies that you give honor to anyone who is in a position of authority.

> *In other words, the best way to teach children to honor you is to demonstrate it as you interact with people whom you honor.*

In other words, the best way to teach children to honor you is to demonstrate it as you interact with people whom you honor.

Guiding children implies a purpose and a goal. It suggests that parents assume responsibility for influencing their children and making learning wholesome and effective.

This responsibility includes the necessity to comprehend the needs of children and to understand how youngsters develop physically and mentally. Your desire to learn about your task and your willingness to risk making mistakes will enable you to study and practice the procedures successfully used by other adults.

As you put your ideas into practice, you will gradually acquire more and more skill in the art of arranging experiences that foster wholesome, happy development. Thereby you will develop understanding and, in time, conviction. The effectiveness of any procedure is limited by the confidence of the adult that he can use it for the child's good. Confidence and conviction will dissipate the fear of breeding hostilities that can misdirect the child throughout life.

> *"The effectiveness of any procedure is limited by the confidence of the adult that he can use it for the child's good."*

A mother asked for help because her ten-year-old had a feeding problem. Questioning revealed that the child came home from school and had unlimited sandwiches, cookies, and fruit before supper. I suggested that she eliminate any eating between meals. The mother was amazed at my suggestion. To her, this would be cruelty. She could still remember how she felt when her mother refused her food. She had tried this and her child cried bitterly. Nevertheless, the fact that the child merely picked at her supper was a source of irritation to both parents. The child was also careless about family routines, such as cleaning her room, which also greatly annoyed her mother. Over a period of time, the mother came to realize that her own response to her child fell far short of the "spectrum of love." Parenthood, to her, was a bothersome task.

Have you ever felt parenthood would be or is a bothersome task? Why?

_____

_____

_____

_____

As the mother saw her own need, she turned to God for His love. After much reassurance, she became bold enough to refuse her child food between meals and insisted that she observe family routines. At times, she resorted to spankings and keeping the child from meeting her friends until her room was clean.

> *"Her success with her child was in proportion to her own development."*

Slowly, the child's resistance yielded under her mother's now friendly, firm supervision. Gradually, the mother grew in understanding of her responsibility and it became a sure conviction. Her success with her child was in proportion to her own development.

APPLICATION (OBEDIENCE TO GOD)

What did God teach me today:

_____

_____

Applying what God is pointing out to you is essential. How will you obey the Lord today?

_____

_____

Write a short prayer to God that summarizes your thoughts.

_____

_____

What are you going to do, say, or think today that will demonstrate obedience to God?

_____

_____

THOUGHT FOR THE DAY
The best way to teach your children to honor you is to demonstrate it as you interact with people you honor.

DAY 4—NON-COMPLIANT BEHAVIOR

Resisting of adult authority is to be expected from children. Paul quoted the psalmist:

As it is written: "There is none righteous, no, not one."
ROMANS 3:10

This natural tendency is faced by all parents. Resistance is a means of control that many children are allowed to use, day in and day out. Some carry this spirit into adulthood without having been taught its true nature and the remedy.

In our experience, children are not at ease when they are "getting away with something." Even a rebellious child is bewildered and disturbed by a parent who indulges his lawlessness, even though he makes it as hard for the parent as possible. Children feel better when definite standards are set up. These are safeguards if they are administered firmly and with kindness.

By non-compliant behavior we mean the opposite of confident expectation.

> *"Children feel better when definite standards are set up."*

Parents teach their children non-compliance without realizing what they are doing.

By non-compliance we mean that the child is given a task and then allowed not to comply with the request. This can happen many times daily.

There are three steps to an avoidance-escape procedure. Some examples:

Request: Time to get up!
Non-compliance: Child doesn't get up.
Outcome: Nothing happens.

Request: Hang up your clothes.
Non-compliance: Child ignores request.
Outcome: Nothing happens.

Request: Eat your peas..
Non-compliance: Child ignores request.
Outcome: Nothing happens.

Request: Close the door.
Non-compliance: Child ignores request.
Outcome: Nothing happens.

Request: Stay seated.
Non-compliance: Child ignores request.
Outcome: Nothing happens.

There are variations to this three step process of non-compliance. The parent may threaten, nag, bluster, explode, or finally, physically assault the child—but seldom follow through to see to it that the child complies with the request.

The child has ways of maintaining non-compliance—whining, crying, yelling, sulking, and tantrums. These responses to a request usually end up with the child not complying with the request.

Non-compliant behavior has predictable consequences:

It hinders peer group relations. Cooperation and learning to give and take are required for children to get along with each other. There needs to be a desire to be in sympathy with the style of the group. A non-compliant child naturally resists the need to comply.

It hinders progress in school. Out of the seat, disrupting the class, and resisting study time results in lower grades and failure to acquire study skills.

Antisocial behavior. Non-compliance leads to fighting, biting, lying, vandalism, aggression, and hyperactivity.

Low self-esteem. It is lonely being a rebel.

Do you really expect your children to behave? Or do they see indulgent smiles that say look how tolerant, how kind, and how understanding I am.

The best way to teach compliance is to demonstrate it. To reign in your own inert impulses, guard your language, and do the right thing at the right time under the scrutiny of your own kids is the toughest test of character and spiritual stamina yet devised.

APPLICATION (OBEDIENCE TO GOD)

What did God teach me today:

_____

_____

Applying what God is pointing out to you is essential. How will you obey the Lord today?

_____

_____

Write a short prayer to God that summarizes your thoughts.

_____

_____

What are you going to do, say, or think today that will demonstrate obedience to God?

_____

_____

> # THOUGHT FOR THE DAY
> ## Non-compliant behavior is a child's method
> ## of controlling the parent.

DAY 5—FAMILY DEVOTIONS

This leads us to something not often thought of as related to discipline—family worship.

This is a time when the family pauses together and worships the Lord. Everywhere we hear that the key to family success is this period that we call the "family devotion." This practice should be carried out steadily and persistently like attendance at school and consistent medical and dental care.

It can be a time when members of the family share questions, doubts, thoughts, problems, and answers. It can be a time of true "togetherness." It can be a time of hearing one another pray, or learning verses of Scripture together. Helping children apply the teaching of the Word to their school subjects makes learning easier and more fun.

In my experience, however, parents speak of the maintenance of the family devotion as a difficult task. The children sometimes resist it. It is difficult to keep interesting. Parents are forever looking for some book or other aid that will make it more attractive.

The success of the family devotions, in my opinion, is a matter of conviction more than a matter of technique or carefully chosen material. The basic question is: "Is it vital to the welfare of your child?"

It is normal for you to see that your child does what you consider important to him. When supper is ready you round up the family regardless of whether they are absorbed in something else. There is no question about your child going to school. If he has trouble with his studies it never occurs to you to let him stay home from classes for a while. You take him to the doctor or dentist even if he screams and you must hold him down. You do not think yourself to be unreasonable or mean. You do not wonder if he will rebel against education or medical or dental care when he is older. You know that as he grows up he will see the need for continuing these practices.

As you consider the family devotions vital to you and your child's welfare, you will see that it is carried out. You will overlook resistance to it as you do in other matters.

Bible reading, the use of devotional books and other materials will be successful only as you consistently carry out this practice with the conviction that it is of vital benefit. It goes without saying that the benefit of the family devotions should be reflected in the relationship of husband and wife and in their spirit toward the children and others. If this is so, you can be assured that your child will not discard a practice or a faith that he finds beneficial to him.

> *"As you consider the family devotions vital to you and your child's welfare, you will see that it is carried out."*

Take time out today to think through and develop your own plan for "Family Devotions and Discipline." Write your plan here.

_____

_____

_____

_____

_____

APPLICATION (OBEDIENCE TO GOD)

What did God teach me today:

_____

_____

Applying what God is pointing out to you is essential. How will you obey the Lord today?

_____

_____

Write a short prayer to God that summarizes your thoughts.

_____

_____

What are you going to do, say, or think today that will demonstrate obedience to God?

_____

_____

THOUGHT FOR THE DAY
Teaching your child to love God through
family devotions is devotion to God.

UNIT 7

DISCIPLINE INVOLVES

SETTING LIMITS

THOUGHT STARTER
Limits provide security for children and their parents.

MEMORY VERSE
"You shall set bounds for the people all around..."
EXODUS 19:12

DAY 1—I HAVE TO SET LIMITS?

If you have the responsibility of getting something done in the family, then it is a matter first of all of setting the limits. This is a job for you and your partner. The rest of your time is spent helping your children observe those limits. How do you get them to want to keep the limits? I do not know. What limits do they want to keep? That is not the question. The question is, what in your considered judgment, is in the best interest of your children? What are reasonable limits that must be observed? They should be reasonable according to your judgment and not according to theirs.

"You shall set bounds for the people all around..."
EXODUS 19:12

What limits have you or do you think you will set for your children? Are they reasonable? Why or why not?

_____

_____

_____

The Perfect Play

There is a football stadium in my home state that holds 100,000 people. Every fall it is filled repeatedly by people who fight traffic jams, are jostled by crushing crowds, suffer through rainstorms, mud, sleet, and snow for several hours.

What is it that provides the magnet for drawing other fans to gather around their television sets at the same time? It is the pleasure and satisfaction that comes from watching eleven men cooperate as one unit to produce in a sudden, dramatic moment a long run, a beautiful pass, or a touchdown!

I have been in the University of Michigan stadium when everyone leaped to his feet at the same time and cheered. What could possibly happen that would cause 100,000 people to do the same thing at the same time? It is the perfect play!

To pull off the perfect play, a player must be willing to subject his own will to a common cause. When it is done right, the perfect play is a beautiful, magical thing to watch.

> *"To pull off the perfect play, a player must be willing to subject his own will to a common cause."*

What makes the perfect play possible is everyone subject to one plan and everyone working together whether it was his idea or not. Each man has his job and can use any legal technique he desires. Every man doing his job…and with flair. That is what creates the perfect play. That is what is beautiful to watch.

Notice, flair is not enough. Every man doing his own thing with flair does not make the perfect play. Everyone has to be working together.

There are some other features about a stadium that draws the people.

1. The size and shape of the playing field is always the same.
2. The way the game is played is governed by the same set of rules.
3. The boundaries that limit the playing area are always the same.
4. The players uniforms are always the same. The school colors do not change.
5. The players are purposed to cooperate under the guidance of a coach.

Refereeing

In a football game, the home and visiting teams even the hometown and visiting fans all go by the same rules and boundaries. These rules are published in a book. You cannot understand the game if you do not know the rules.

> *"You cannot understand the game if you do not know the rules."*

Making sure the players stay within the limits is the job of the officials. If a player breaks a limit, the referee penalizes the team. The player and his team have to accept the consequences.

That is no big deal. You just take your consequences and the game goes on. If you protest too much, and get kicked out of the game, the crowd may approve. The referee's interpretation of the game is final. If you argue with the official you get kicked out of the game, not off the team. Remember kicked out of the game, not life.

Your Limits Make You Unique

The word "football" tells you many things. It settles the shape of the ball, the dimensions of the playing field, the rules of the game, even the clothes you wear.

The word "family" also tells you many things. Your limits make you unique. If we use a name, say the Landrum family, it tells you many things about the choices that family made about how things should go.

Mr. and Mrs. Landrum are the ones to make those choices. When they do, the word Landrum will mean something to them as a family. Translated into a list, it would look something like this:

- your address
- type of house
- your church
- your school
- style of recreation
- meal time
- table manners
- entertaining at home

- television time
- how you dress
- how you handle your clothes
- house rules
- choice of toys
- neatness
- contact with friends

A closer look at the Landrum family allows us to observe some specific limits.

1. Eat a balanced meal.
2. Don't eat crackers or other such food on the living room couch.
3. Pick up your toys when you are through with them.
4. Hang up your clothes.
5. The family sits together at church.
6. Each child has a regular bedtime.

Do these sound reasonable? There are many more you could add to your list. Some you could change or eliminate. From preschool age on up, limits are necessary. In the home or neighborhood the smallest children need certain limits pertaining to safety, sharing, destroying, hurting others, taking turns, and respecting others' feelings.

Remember, limits give you a basis for dealing with your children. If you are consistent, then it helps your children to know what to expect from you. Limits alone though will not transform children into obedient people.

> *"Remember, limits give you a basis for dealing with your children."*

Setting limits will not deal with the problem of human nature—the sinfulness of your children. Limits will not change children's attitudes, or their spirit. Limits will reveal attitudes and spirit.

By setting limits:
1. you allow your children some freedom of choice,
2. you make things a little more predictable, and
3. you provide a framework for dealing with your children.

APPLICATION (OBEDIENCE TO GOD)

What did God teach me today:

_____

_____

Applying what God is pointing out to you is essential. How will you obey the Lord today?

_____

_____

Write a short prayer to God that summarizes your thoughts.

_____

_____

What are you going to do, say, or think today that will demonstrate obedience to God?

_____

_____

THOUGHT FOR THE DAY
Limits give you a basis for dealing with your children.

DAY 2—DISCIPLINE INVOLVES HELP

It should be understood that children will never maintain limits perfectly. Parents often ask, "How often must I tell that child to behave?" The answer is, "Constantly." Children have their ups and downs just as adults do. However, the preschool child does make a beginning toward accepting limits. For example, a teacher was showing a three-year-old boy the meaning of sharing toys with other children. Sometime later she was looking on as he and another boy were playing together. The three-year-old slipped up to the other child, who was playing with a little car, grabbed it out of his hand, and said, "Let's share." He had misunderstood the concept of sharing.

What would you do in this situation?

_____

_____

_____

_____

_____

He needed some careful teaching, not a scolding. The teacher had to go to the boy and in a very gentle and firm manner say, "You must give it back. When he is through with the car, you may have it." The boy did not want to give it back, but his playmate also had his rights. The car was to be shared only after his playmate had kept it for a reasonable time. The teacher firmly took the car away from the protesting child and returned it to the child who had it first. She led the reluctant child away to find something else to play with.

Help In Applying The Rule

You can give a child a simple rule or a simple reason. You do not need to repeat that reason twenty times. What your child needs is a little help in applying the rule. Children learn by doing. A child will remember 90% of what he hears, sees, and touches and 10% of what he hears. In the case of the two small boys, this help meant taking the car from one boy and giving it back to his playmate. The offender in this situation did not need to be punished; he did need to be helped.

> "The offender in this situation did not need to be punished; he did need to be helped."

You must work with your children in the spirit of a helpful teacher. Remember that everything is not taught in one day. You have many years to train your children. This necessitates understanding and consistency, gentleness, and fairness. Adults are still struggling with some of these principles of right living. You cannot expect your children to become perfect overnight. Children value their possessions as much as you do yours.

> "Children value their possessions much as we do ours."

It is easy for us to tell them to share their toys, but how freely do we share our lawn mower or our automobile?

_____

_____

The Game

So, now it is time to set limits for the family. Think of it. The two people in all the world who care the most about your children, you and your partner, are planning the finest possible life for them.

Doesn't that sound great? What could be more fun than two parents deciding what is best for the children?

Limits: A Field To Play On

In our family, we looked at limits as areas of freedom...of choice of activities. For example, we had designated certain areas for play. In the living room, you could read or play the record player.

In the family room, you could play with remote control cars, toys, or games. The only limitation was, put the game or toy back when you get through.

There were even some things you could do in the kitchen. You could always help with the dishes. You could help scrape a carrot, peel potatoes, or help bake cookies. Mom made all these tasks fun. Or you could sit at the table and talk to her.

Then there was the basement. You had many choices down there—a swing...screwed to the rafters—a tricycle and a wagon.

The real attraction was a piano box, which, on one day would serve as a skyscraper, the next day as a submarine, the following day a house. You could make anything out of it you wanted.

There was a bench, with a hammer and nails, and a saw. Wood was cut to size so you could nail pieces together.

Outside, there was a swing set, which had a swing, parallel bars, and rings. There was another wagon. And a sandbox...full of toys.

In all these activity areas, the only limitations were that you (1) did not throw things or (2) hit anyone. You must take your turn. You could make all the noise you wanted in these areas except for the living room and the family room. These were conversation rooms.

The limits defined the options. The children learn to make choices within the limits. They begin to respect the rights of others.

> "The limits defined the options."

What limits do you or will you have for your children?

_____

_____

_____

_____

A Framework For Dealing With Your Child

Tony discovered this after going out of his way to set what he thought was a reasonable limit with his eleven-year old son. He even got his son to participate in making the decision.

"Let's set a reasonable limit, son."

Before supper, you wash your hands.

His son agreed. "Yes, Dad, that's reasonable."

Until just before supper it was reasonable. Then the child suddenly disagreed with Dad. After all, his hands were not that dirty, and he was hungry and ready for supper. Dad firmly marched his son to a sink and saw to it that his son washed his hands. That is helping his son stay within the limit.

Suppose you have three children. The preschooler goes to bed at 7:30, the grade schooler at 8:30, and the junior high child at 10:00. Now, there is much creativity possible in order to get them to bed.

But at night, bedtime is bedtime. And not "oh, just this one more TV program" time. There is no question about when the child goes to bed. It does not matter if it is Mom or Dad doing the job.

What approach do you take to make sure the limits are kept? That is up to you. Do it however you want. But do it. Help them!

Remember the magnet that draws people into the football stadium. It is the thrill and satisfaction of watching eleven men cooperate to produce a sudden, dramatic run, a beautiful pass, or the perfect touchdown play.

Parenthood is like that. Its fascination comes in working together to pull off a pleasant meal, an evening marked by the cheery laughter of happy children, or getting all three of them to bed smoothly, easily, happily.

The perfect play does not happen very often, but you keep trying, cooperating, working together—within the limits you are both committed to.

A Miracle?

There is a day to day variation of how much energy it takes for you to do your job. To accept responsibility for getting the children to bed is half the battle. Usually, the preschooler is the first barrier. But not tonight. This time, it is different for a change.

You just scoop him up and put him to bed. Phew, that was easy for once.

The grade school child provides more of a challenge. She varies from night to night. Some nights, she goes to bed at your first suggestion, and other nights, she is so worn out, she just disappears. Then another evening might find her full of vim and vigor and nowhere near ready to go to bed.

Tonight she just disappears.

Two down and one to go.

Usually your junior higher resists bedtime. So it takes more creativity to help her meet her limit. Some nights she would be willing to discuss the merits of going to bed or anything else, just to avoid going to bed.

But tonight—no problem. You did it. The perfect play.

Those Vim And Vigor Nights

On those vim and vigor nights, you might want to set up a race around the block, giving the smallest children big head starts. Maybe a relaxing bath is the best thing. Possibly you may want to calm your child down by reading him a book. Do whatever is necessary.

"Oh...no!" you say. "That's too much work." Well, a healthy, busy child will create more work for you on those active nights. You want a busy, healthy child. Still, bedtime is bedtime.

On such nights, do not expect perfect plays. Just figure on a little more time and effort that both husband and wife will have to put forth.

Your willingness to stick to bedtime might be creating challenges for you. Your teenager is alert, full of vim and vigor. She is a busy, good student. One of the reasons might be that she gets enough sleep. She's well rested. Your own good administration makes getting a teenager to bed on time a creative effort.

The task varies from night to night, but the limits stay the same.

APPLICATION (OBEDIENCE TO GOD)

What did God teach me today:

_____

_____

Applying what God is pointing out to you is essential. How will you obey the Lord today?

_____

_____

Write a short prayer to God that summarizes your thoughts.

_____

_____

What are you going to do, say, or think today that will demonstrate obedience to God?

_____

_____

THOUGHT FOR THE DAY
Children need help to apply the rules.

DAY 3—CHILDREN ARE PEOPLE TOO!

What about their attitudes? Will limits ruin them emotionally? We are talking about guiding children, not changing their spirit. They get their joy from God—just as you do.

They are people, just like you. Remember what people are like:

For the good that I will to do, I do not do; but the evil
I will not to do, that I practice.
ROMANS 7:19

We have turned, every one, to his own way...
ISAIAH 53:6

Your children need a Savior, too. They have the same drives you do. That is why their Christian education is important. That is why it is a twenty-year job.

Limits Provide Security

I did not think too much about it the evening my daughter approached me just as I was ready to walk up on the platform.

"Hey, Dad, could I have the keys to the car? After the meeting I want to take a carload of kids up to Santa Cruz."

"O.K.," I said, without thinking.

Then I went to the platform to make my speech about how important it is for a man and his wife to be agreed on limits and be committed to them. After I finished the speech I went to a large foyer in the back of the auditorium. There were hundreds of people milling around back there.

My daughter came to me with her carload of friends behind her and said, "Dad, I want the keys now."

My wife was standing there and she said, "I told you you couldn't go."

Well, there were some people standing around who heard us. They started assembling another little congregation there to see how the speaker would handle this.

How would you handle this situation?

_____

_____

_____

You cannot think of everything, especially when you are traveling. But we had a limit at our house that said the first parent you ask, that is it. All I had to do was to find out whom she had asked first. It turned out she had asked her mother first.

This is what you call "testing the limits." You can expect your children to pick times like that to do it. You see, I had to make a decision quickly. Will we raise children or save face? We were committed to raising children. So I said to my daughter, "You know the answer. You asked your mother first."

> Her response was, "But Dad, you are embarrassing me in front of all these people."

Her response was, "But Dad, you are embarrassing me in front of all these people."

Now this is a child putting pressure on you, isn't it? I am embarrassing her in front of all these people. I want to point out that for her not to get the car when she knew perfectly well what the limit was, and for us to hold to the limit, is security, dependability. This is refereeing. It is crucial and important that your children realize their mother and father set limits and can be depended on to carry them out.

Bargaining

I listened to a story in the consulting room that points up the need for commitment to the family plan. The parents brought their boy to see me because he was smoking and could not be trusted. The parents were concerned about it, and they made a deal with him.

"If you promise to quit smoking, we will buy you a bicycle."

"It's a deal."

So they bought him a bicycle, but it was not long before they realized he was smoking again.

"If you will quit smoking," they said, "we will send you to your favorite summer camp."

"It's a deal"—again without hesitation. When he came home from summer camp they discovered he was smoking again. Finally, at this point, they brought him to me because they were concerned they had a son who would not keep his word. They did not trust him.

I had a talk with the boy and this is what I found out. His father had an idea that you should not have ice cream during the day. Frequently this boys' mother would pick the kids up from school, and they would stop to get an ice cream sundae.

The only stipulation was—do not tell Dad.

There was something else the boy told me. These people went to a church where one of the standards you accepted when you joined the church was that you would not drink alcoholic beverages. Dad liked a good cold beer when he came home from work, but he got everyone to promise that "mum's the word" when it came to his beer.

Where did this young fellow get the idea of making an agreement and then breaking it? It is obvious he observed it from his father and mother. These people pretended they were accepting some limits and then went ahead and broke them. Why should the boy make a little deal with Dad, and then not intend to keep it? Where did he get the idea? The example was mother and father. When you set a limit it must be binding on everybody in the family.

> *"You see these were people who pretended that they were accepting some limits and then went ahead and broke them."*

You can expect your children to resist your limits and test them.

APPLICATION (OBEDIENCE TO GOD)

What did God teach me today:

_____

_____

Applying what God is pointing out to you is essential. How will you obey the Lord today?

_____

_____

Write a short prayer to God that summarizes your thoughts.

_____

_____

What are you going to do, say, or think today that will demonstrate obedience to God?

_____

_____

THOUGHT FOR THE DAY
Provide security through limits even though your children will resist and test them.

DAY 4—DEFINITION OF FREEDOM

There is the possibility that no matter how reasonable a limit is, in your judgment, your children will not agree that it provides them with reasonable freedom. Remember, you are the leaders, not your children.

What is freedom? I like this definition—Freedom is the length of a leash from a chosen stake. Picture that. The leash can be short or long. It can be adjusted. There is a lot of freedom between the stake and the outer boundary. When it comes to children you can give them more or less freedom, depending on how they handle it. Freedom can be adjusted.

I once was driving on a highway in Texas, and my companion said to me, "You are now on the biggest ranch in the entire world." It was so big that the highway we were traveling along ran through the ranch, like a big driveway. Along the road were fences to keep livestock in. There were many cows behind those fences—and they had incredible freedom. Why you could not even see the other fences that kept them on this ranch. The fences were so far away they were over the horizon.

Some kind of freedom! Yet, wouldn't you know, there was one cow straining her neck through the fence to get a blade of grass on the other side. The cow had acres to choose from. Yet it opted for an unattainable space covering just a few inches.

> "No matter how broad the limits are, your children will test the limits."

I thought—how much like people. No matter how broad the limits, your children will test the limits.

The limits set in any family should be mutually agreeable to both the father and the mother; otherwise, children learn to play off one parent against the other.

Write your most recent memory of a child playing one parent against the other.

_____

_____

_____

To illustrate, at a banquet in a church one evening Jimmy whispered to his mother, "May I go to the car and play the radio?" "No, you may not!" she replied. So Jimmy watched until his mother was engaged in conversation. He then quietly turned to his father and said, "How about the keys to the car, Dad, so I can go out and listen to the radio?" Without thinking, Dad reached in his pocket, gave his son the keys, and Jimmy disappeared outside. When Dad and Mom came to themselves and

> "...whenever one person's life crosses another there must be some definite understanding so that the relationship may develop smoothly."

realized what had happened, they had to admit that they were not thinking alike. The older children become, the more clever they are in pitting one parent against the other. Therefore, it is important that from the early stages of your marriage you accept the fact that whenever one person's life crosses another there must be some definite understanding so that the relationship may develop smoothly.

Limits And Neighbors

When it comes to training children, the responsibility for carrying out limits lies with the parent. The character and the understanding of the parent are much more trustworthy than the understanding of the child.

The following experience of one parent illustrates the fact that your limits may not be appreciated by your children and seemingly are not always appreciated by the neighbors.

This parent felt that her child should not cross the busy highway on his bicycle. The other parents in the neighborhood said to their children, "If the rest of the mothers say their child can do it, you can do it."

The gang would go to this woman's house and plead, but she would say, "No! you can't do it."

Her child was distraught. "Everybody else's mother says we can go. You always keep us from going."

Suppose this were your family. How would you respond?

_____

_____

_____

_____

After this happened a few times, the children went once again with the same request. All the other mothers said they could go. Finally, the harassed mother yielded to the pressure and let them go. Suddenly she was hailed as a wonderful mother because the children could have their way. The children had hardly gotten started when the telephone rang. One of the neighbors had called, saying, "Did you tell the children they could cross the street?" "Why, yes." The neighbor replied, "We were depending on you not to let your child go."

To have a happy home you may hold standards or values that will seem odd to the neighbors; or your neighbors may silently respect you. In either case, you had better do what is right before God, not what is right in your child's eyes, or perhaps in the eyes of the mother next door. If the mother next door does not like this, you still

> *"To have a happy home you may hold standards or values that will seem odd to the neighbors..."*

must be pleasant to her—from your heart. This requires complete consecration and yieldedness to God.

Limits Outside The Home

It is important for small children to have supervised contacts outside the home. This is important because limits outside the home are different from those within the home. Adults outside the family will react differently also. A child's first attempts to approach other children or his reactions to being approached by other children are usually similar to those at home. If he is accustomed to taking what he wants, asking for what he wants, or looking longingly at what he wants, he will do so outside the home. However, the response to his approach by other children or adults may be different from what he is accustomed to at home. His approach, successful at home, may be unsuccessful outside the home.

> *"...successful at home, may be unsuccessful outside the home."*

To illustrate, a four-year-old girl, the only child in the family, and the pride and joy of her parents, went to nursery school. She had learned her manners well. Whenever she wanted something, she would say, "Please, may I have it?" Her parents would then grant her most of her requests. At school she walked up to a little girl nearby and said, "Please, may I have that doll?" "No," was the answer. The four-year-old returned to her mother with a puzzled look on her face and explained," I said please, and she won't give it to me." The mother, too, looked puzzled. The teacher told the mother and child that what might be a successful approach in the home would not necessarily work outside the home. The other child had rights also. It is important that a young child have such contacts at her own age level outside the home, so that she can learn the facts of life, four-year-old style.

APPLICATION (OBEDIENCE TO GOD)

What did God teach me today:

_____

_____

Applying what God is pointing out to you is essential. How will you obey the Lord today?

_____

_____

Write a short prayer to God that summarizes your thoughts.

_____

_____

What are you going to do, say, or think today that will demonstrate obedience to God?

_____

_____

THOUGHT FOR THE DAY
No matter how broad the limits,
your child will test them.

DAY 5—ADULTS HAVE LIMITS TOO!

The following excerpts are from a father's letter written to his son at graduation time. Though written as humor, it conveys a vital message:

Dear Son,

I'm sure you are thrilled by the idea of taking your place at last in adult affairs—a station of life you probably look upon as a time when "big people" will stop telling you to do things...or not to do things...Your dad has found out that the chains of adult life are wrought of stiffer stuff than the feeble fetters of childhood. Believe me, no one ever suffered a furrowed brow from such simple commands as "Eat your cereal"...Do your homework"...Report for band practice." What once may have seemed a terribly harsh order, "Put away your comic book," will pale into insignificance when compared with "Cut out all pastries and sweets."

The bigger you get, the bigger other people seem to get—if not bigger in stature, then bigger in authority. For example, did you see the look on dad's face when the Internal Revenue man ordered him to report to the collector's office with all of his 1957 tax receipts?...When a traffic officer says, "Pull over to the curb," dad pulls over. When grandmother says, "Roll up the window," dad rolls up the window...I just want to prepare you for a lifetime of saying, "Yes, sir" to master sergeants, shop foremen, loan company executives, bank tellers, tradesmen, public officials, car dealers, game wardens, and a host of other people you never dreamed were your superiors. Even the most politely phrased commands, like "Please remit," or "Kindly step back in the bus," are still commands. Ushers will order you down an aisle; headwaiters will tell you where to sit; courts will summon you for jury duty, the city hall will notify you to shovel the snow off your sidewalk.

You will be dragged off to parties at other people's houses, and dragged out of bed by people who come to your house. You will be kept off the grass by policemen and kept up by weekend guests. You will be put on committees and put off streetcars. This is the true life beyond commencement. Congratulations and good luck.

Dad
PS Get a haircut for graduation.

The job of setting limits is not an arena for unresolved arguments between parents. One set for mom and another set for dad will not do. Setting limits involves a commitment of both parents to the same limits.

> *"The job of setting limits is not an arena for unresolved arguments between parents."*

Describe the limits you have versus your spouse's limits for the children.

_____

_____

_____

_____

_____

The leadership of the family comes into play here. All stalemates between parents need to be settled. The question of who has the last word will arise and must be settled. It is in this area where the wife may well have the most input and experience. The husband should consider her views carefully before he overrules his wife, assuming she is the one who spends most of the time dealing with the children.

If the wife works or has outside activities, careful planning between parents over the division of responsibilities is obvious. Then a strategy for dealing with the children in the evening saves many debates between parents and gives the children a sense of stability and family cooperation.

Limits Should Have The Following Characteristics:
• They should help a child know what is expected of him.
• They should be reachable, reasonable, and clearly understood...those that the child is able to achieve and that the child might even enjoy working toward.
• They should provide a framework for dealing with your children.
• They must allow some freedom of choice.
• There should be as few of them as possible.
Setting limits calls for experts. You are the experts.

Now, how do you carry out these limits?

The setting of limits is inherent in the need for authority and security. Just as God sets limits for us and enforces them by chastisement, so should we with our children. The setting of intelligent, thoughtful, reasonable limits is a God delegated duty—limits that are in line with the needs of the child and appropriate to his age, understanding, and moral values.

> *"The setting of intelligent, thoughtful, reasonable limits is a God delegated duty..."*

Take time to discuss today's material with your spouse. Spend an evening together agreeing on limits for your children. Write the results here:

_____

_____

_____

_____

_____

_____

APPLICATION (OBEDIENCE TO GOD)

What did God teach me today:

_____

_____

Applying what God is pointing out to you is essential. How will you obey the Lord today?

_____

_____

Write a short prayer to God that summarizes your thoughts.

_____

_____

What are you going to do, say, or think today that will demonstrate obedience to God?

_____

_____

THOUGHT FOR THE DAY
Limits that provide security is a God-delegated
duty for parents.

UNIT 8

DISCIPLINE INVOLVES HELP

THOUGHT STARTER
You may have to help your child obey.

MEMORY VERSE
And a servant of the Lord must not quarrel but be gentle to all, able to teach, patient, in humility correcting those who are in opposition, if God perhaps will grant them repentance, so that they may know the truth.
2 TIMOTHY 2:24-25

DAY 1—YOUR JOB DESCRIPTION

A lifeguard may be sitting up in his lifeguard chair comfortable and sunning himself. If a swimmer suddenly needs his help, the lifeguard should not consider this an interruption. These swimmers are his primary responsibility.

Parents need to consider children as their primary responsibility, not as interruptions.

Now...wait a minute. Parents have needs, too, don't they? They need time to fulfill their personal needs, don't they? Of course they do. So do waitresses, lifeguards, businessmen, coaches, athletes, secretaries, teachers, and everyone else.

Responsibility with appropriate authority is an important part of personal fulfillment. Creating the limits, revising them when necessary, expending the energy to work within the limits, and interacting with one another is part of the joy of living.

Of course, there are coffee breaks, rest periods, substitutes, and days off. Work takes energy. Interacting with people is tiring. There are good days and there are bad days. There are easy days and there are tough days. One day you have happy customers and another day it seems they are all grumpy.

Take the referee as an example. He keeps the game going smoothly. He is expected to call the plays according to the limits, to be impartial, consistent, and cool-headed. His job can be tough or easy on any given day, depending on the mood of the players, their skill, the importance of the game, and even the weather. Some days there are few close calls and few penalties. Other days, there can be some debatable, close calls and many penalties.

Referees rise to the demands of the game. He is in on every play. Some games require more effort and others less, but the limits do not change. Refereeing does not interfere with his personal fulfillment. It is part of it. He does not bemoan the fact that he is not a spectator. He relishes the job.

Like refereeing, guiding children can be a tough job or an easy job on any given day. It depends on the mood of the children, who they are with, the importance of the problems that come up, and even the weather. Some days all goes smoothly. No one is stepping over the limits or challenging the calls. Other days you blow the whistle constantly and are called upon to make some debatable decisions.

Decisions do not change the limits. You rise to the demands of the day. Guiding children is not something that interferes with your personal life—it is part of it. The wholesome parent does not bemoan the job, but relishes it.

> *"Guiding children is not something that interferes with your personal life—it is part of it."*

Parenting goes back to a matter of the Spirit. I am reminded of a pithy Bible passage:

And whatever you do, do it heartily, as to the Lord and not to men, knowing that from the Lord you will receive the reward of the inheritance; for you serve the Lord Jesus Christ. But he who does wrong will be repaid for the wrong which he has done, and there is no partiality.
COLOSSIANS 3:23-25

How about a play on former President Kennedy's words: Ask not what the family can do for you; ask rather what you can do for the family.

If a businessman plays tennis, he must provide for the supervision of his business while away from the office. If a parent plays tennis, he must provide for the supervision of his children during that time. In either case, whether it be the businessman or the parent, the substitute supervisor is guided by the same limits you would use.

Let me return to the statement, "parents have to consider children their primary responsibility, not interruptions." Gwen learned this:

> It hardly ever failed. All I had to do was to sit down for a TV show in the evening, and my five-year-old would come up asking me to read The Lion, the Witch, and the Wardrobe, or some other story book.
>
> I resented it—until I realized my TV watching was like the lifeguard getting a suntan. My primary responsibility was to the children.
>
> So I changed my viewpoint. If I sit down to watch a TV program with children around, I do so expecting to be interrupted. Sometimes I ask my

child to wait, or offer some alternative activities until the program is over, or shift him over to dad. Most of the time, something works.

Otherwise, I put off my TV watching until all the children are in bed—with one exception.

Tuesday night at 8 o'clock, my favorite TV show airs. On that night my husband takes the major responsibilities of the evening so I can have that one pleasure...undisturbed and unbothered.

Overall, my kids come first. I am their mother and want to be available."

Sam came to the same realization.

The Saturday or Sunday football game would come on, and I'd sit down to watch it. Like clockwork, here would come my son Jess, age five, with his football, wanting to play catch in the backyard.

At first, it bugged me, and I tried to put him off. Then I realized I had bought him the football. Also, it was a chance to do some teaching.

"I'll play with you for fifteen minutes," I tell him now. That's about all his interest and energy span will allow for. It's time for fellowship and helping Jeff learn how to handle a football.

So I start out my afternoons planning to play football in the backyard. After we're done and Jess is tired or wants to go to another activity, I sit down and watch the rest of the game. Since the ball game lasts three hours, this doesn't always work out. Jeff may be back.

Let me toss in a serious question here.

Am I asking parents to overindulge their children? Why or why not?

_____

_____

_____

Well, take a look at the last two examples. Both children involved are five-year-olds. You must do something with them, even if it interferes with your plans. Children will not evaporate.

The presence or actions of a child demands a response whether you like it or not. I reported the choices Gwen and Sam made. Whatever you and your partner agree on, do it with all your heart.

> *"Whatever you and your partner agree on, do it with all your heart."*

If you have any doubt about your choices, then consult with some parents whom you respect. The important point here is that your children are entitled to the best judgment available

121

on their behalf and some serious, happy effort on your part in putting your judgment into action.

Enjoyable Parenthood

Isn't it strange that dedicated parents at times resist their job just as children resist limits? Half the battle in parenthood is accepting the task and the never-ending surprises and frustrations that children bring to the job.

APPLICATION (OBEDIENCE TO GOD)

What did God teach me today:

_____

_____

Applying what God is pointing out to you is essential. How will you obey the Lord today?

_____

_____

Write a short prayer to God that summarizes your thoughts.

_____

_____

What are you going to do, say, or think today that will demonstrate obedience to God?

_____

_____

THOUGHT FOR THE DAY
**Dedicated parents at times resist their job
just as children resist their parents' limits.**

DAY 2—THE PRINCIPLE OF HELP

To make parenthood easier and more enjoyable, here are five suggestions lumped together under a concept called help.

Help is assisting your child to get the best results from any effort put forth. Here are at least five ways of helping a child:

1. Redirecting unacceptable behavior.

2. Giving help as needed.

3. Giving more help than needed.

4. Preparing situations in advance.

5. Pressure.

Redirecting

I recall a scene in a friend's home.

There were four children in the television room, and the limit was...no horseplay. One of the smaller children was in an ugly mood that morning, and she was going around pestering the other children.

How should a mother handle that?

_____

_____

_____

The little girl woke up in a bad mood and was making herself obnoxious. What was the simplest way to handle her? To swat her one would make a worse mess. So mother moved into the TV room and said, "Let's have some breakfast."

She bodily removed her daughter, plunked her in front of the table, and fed her something. All the girl needed was some help in behaving herself. Tomorrow she might be cooperative. Today she was a problem. Feeding her worked. If it had not, mother would have to try something else.

> *"Parents have twenty years to raise children. You need not make a crisis on any one day."*

Do you follow me? Parents have twenty years to raise children. You need not make a crisis on any one day. This mother made her task as easy on herself as she could. She enforced the limit. The moody child was not allowed to bother the children in the television room. She simply was removed until she could get over her nasty mood.: This is an example of a mother redirecting unacceptable behavior.

Redirecting often is the answer to settling a dispute. If two children are fighting over a bicycle, the best solution might be redirecting their attention and energy somewhere else.

"Put the bike in the garage. Here's a football."

"Go and play ping pong."

If you are ready with a list of alternatives you make your job easier. This is redirecting.

APPLICATION (OBEDIENCE TO GOD)

What did God teach me today:

_____

_____

Applying what God is pointing out to you is essential. How will you obey the Lord today?

_____

_____

Write a short prayer to God that summarizes your thoughts.

_____

_____

What are you going to do, say, or think today that will demonstrate obedience to God?

_____

_____

THOUGHT FOR THE DAY
Do not make a crisis out of one event or one day.

DAY 3—GIVING HELP

I was in a home one time...in the living room. A little boy was in the family room shouting, "I hate these filthy old things." We looked in to find a small child throwing blocks. He was frustrated because he could not stack the blocks. His father moved in quickly and grabbed his hand, saying, "You can't throw blocks."

Then Dad quieted the boy down by just holding him. They sat on the floor together. Dad took two blocks and said, "Move the two closer together. Now you put one on top. Move it like this." He picked up four blocks for the child who then carried on himself, and we went back into the living room. No crisis. Isn't that simple?

It is like the little girl pulling her wagon along the sidewalk, only to have it slip off and get stuck. The child begins to scream. Her mother came on the scene, sees the problem and helps the child pull the wagon back up on the sidewalk, saying, "You were too close to the edge."

All the child needed was a little help, a single demonstration, some kind of explanation.

Giving More Help Than Needed

This type of assistance is given in spite of the fact the child can do the task. Just to make it more fun, the parent becomes a partner and pitches in with the child.

Loreen's family had a rule about the family room. She had to clean it up every night before she went to bed.

She could do the job by herself. She had the ability. Her father noted that the job was distasteful to Loreen, so he became her cleaning partner for a while. Together, they picked up the blocks, one holding the box, the other putting them in.

As a team, they stacked the books and put the toys in the toy box. They straightened up the rocking horse and put all the furniture in the proper position.

Cleaning the family room was a fun time of the day all because a father became a partner parent. This help enabled a child to get personal pleasure as well as satisfaction from doing a job.

Assistance is especially effective when a child faces jobs that are long and hard, or jobs that are scheduled at "tired" times of the day.

When Loreen's father first started helping her with the nightly pickup, he understandably picked up most of the debris. As the days went by, he picked up less and less.

Ultimately, all he needed to do every night was to remind her to pick up the family room. She breezed through the job by herself. Occasionally, he watched her or helped her.

Loreen's father helped her keep the limits. Yet he avoided the rigidity of another father who had the same rule. Every night, he went flying through the house, "Where is that girl? She knows she is to clean up the family room every night. It's her responsibility. She's going to do it! Right now!"

This father was not being very creative. It is easy to see that this is not a helping atmosphere.

APPLICATION (OBEDIENCE TO GOD)

What did God teach me today:

_____

_____

Applying what God is pointing out to you is essential. How will you obey the Lord today?

_____

_____

Write a short prayer to God that summarizes your thoughts.

_____

_____

What are you going to do, say, or think today that will demonstrate obedience to God?

_____

_____

> ## THOUGHT FOR THE DAY
> ### Teach your child by giving help joyfully.

DAY 4—PREPARING IN ADVANCE

This type of help is used by a parent who understands his child's abilities and limitations and anticipates when the child is ready for new experiences. The child may not even be aware of them.

By making conditions favorable in advance, the parent helps the child discover new abilities. Such help may be unseen and even unknown by the child, but it often is most effective.

To prepare in advance, the parent must take his cues from his children. Watch your child for inclinations, interests, and special abilities. From these, you decide how you are going to assist.

> *To prepare in advance, the parent must take his cues from his children.*

Through preparation in advance, you develop your child's abilities. You do this from day one. You can buy crib toys and tie them to the crib so your baby can amuse himself. Later on you decide your child may be interested in blocks. You buy some and put them out for him to play with. The same is done with the crayons, push-pull toys, puzzles, and other activities.

Watch for the developing interests of your child. You prepare the way for him.

Preparation in advance can guide a child's day. When a child wakes up, his blocks, a book, or a puzzle is set out for him. You can guide your child's activity through this sort of help.

Preparing conditions in advance can help in developing self-confidence in your child.

Purchasing a ball and bat and taking time to play with your child is an example. Providing a sewing machine and leaving easy projects around makes it easy for your daughter to get interested.

> "Preparing conditions in advance can help in developing self-confidence in your child."

Leaving easy to read, interesting books around may stimulate reading. Leaving audio and video tapes of your choosing may stimulate an interest in music.

"There's Nothing to Do!"

Advance preparation helps the parent if he is ready with a list of suggestions. Sometime in your life you have heard these words (or will hear them), "Mom...I don't have anything to do?" A parent can be ready with several alternatives prepared and analyzed in advance.

"Why don't you go out and play on the swing?"

"I don't wanna."

"Why don't you go downstairs and play on the horse?"

"I don't wanna."

"Why don't you help me with the dishes?"

"I don't wanna."

"Why don't you go read one of your new Little House books?"

"Oh...O.K."

Advance preparations give the child a choice.

One father I talked to pointed out, "I don't let my daughter go out with any non-Christians."

"Oh?"

"Right. And I don't let my daughter..."

On he continued until I got the impression that he had given his daughter a list of activities she could not do. My impression turned out to be true. He had not given her any suggestions on what she could do.

He had not done anything about providing her with some Christian boys to date.

The next time your teenager comes to you and grumbles, "Good grief! There's nothing to do around here. This place is dead!" What will be your reaction? Have a list of choices for him.

"Well, you can invite the youth group over Sunday."

"You can ride your bike."

"You can go to the YMCA."

"You can go to the gym."

"You can play ping-pong in the basement."

"You can play table games."

"You can invite your friends in."

"You can listen to records."

"You can put this kit together."

APPLICATION (OBEDIENCE TO GOD)

What did God teach me today:

_____

_____

Applying what God is pointing out to you is essential. How will you obey the Lord today?

_____

_____

Write a short prayer to God that summarizes your thoughts.

_____

_____

What are you going to do, say, or think today that will demonstrate obedience to God?

_____

_____

THOUGHT FOR THE DAY
Teach your child by preparing in advance.

DAY 5—PRESSURE AS HELP

At times, parents need to use pressure. Suppose it is time to go to church and your child does not want to go. It does not help much to say, "If you don't go, I'll whack you."

What kind of pressure gets him to church? You lock arms and march your child to the car. That is pressure.

One parent asked, "What do I do when my child sneaks out of church?" If they sneak out, then next time have them sit beside you.

They will probably say, "What's the matter? Don't you trust me?"

> *"What kind of pressure gets him to church? You lock arms and march your child to the car. That's pressure."*

The answer is, "No. I can't be sure what you will do when left out of my sight."

I was in a Sunday school department one day, where a boy, ten or eleven years old, was throwing spit balls at some other children. I heard the teacher say, "I wouldn't do that if I were you." The boy just ignored the teacher and kept up his activity.

Another adult, perhaps the director, came in and observed what was going on. He moved in on the boy, sat him down in his chair and said, "That's enough."

The boy looked up at the man and the man looked down at the boy. The little boy looked at his teacher, and his teacher looked at the man, who just shrugged his shoulders and walked away, but kept an eye on the boy.

The boy needed some pressure from a confident adult. Even the child was smart enough to realize the man made a sensible decision.

1. Redirecting often is the simplest way to handle unacceptable behavior and conflict between children.

2. Giving help as needed is the kind of help the child most frequently needs to accomplish a task.

3. Giving more help than needed probably is the most fun, where parent becomes partner. It ensures personal pleasure and satisfaction when a child is doing a task.

4. Preparing in advance helps you keep a child busy or introduces him to new activities.

5. Pressure is the most dramatic and most misunderstood type of help. Yet it helps a child know what is expected of him, even if unpleasant, and ultimately encourages him in a path of independence. Use it carefully.

Loving guidance is rewarding both to the child and to the parent. Remember the promise:

> **Train up a child in the way he should go, And when he is old he will not depart from it.**
> PROVERBS 22:6

> *"Help involves continuous daily effort."*

Help involves continuous daily effort. If you view each daily incident with your children as part of a twenty-year plan and not a crisis of the moment, you have a good start on the proper use of help.

Lend your child a helping hand.

APPLICATION (OBEDIENCE TO GOD)

What did God teach me today:

_____

_____

Applying what God is pointing out to you is essential. How will you obey the Lord today?

_____

_____

Write a short prayer to God that summarizes your thoughts.

_____

_____

What are you going to do, say, or think today that will demonstrate obedience to God?

_____

_____

THOUGHT FOR THE DAY
Help involves continual daily effort.

UNIT 9

DEALING WITH RESISTANCE

THOUGHT STARTER
Children know how to test their parent's hearts—resist.

MEMORY VERSE
If you are willing and obedient, You shall eat the good of the land;
But if you refuse and rebel, You shall be devoured...
ISAIAH 1:19, 20

DAY 1—THE FACT OF RESISTANCE

Question: How is it that our children resist some of our limits after we worked so hard to make them reasonable and reachable?

Remember the essence of human nature:

We have turned, every one, to his own way...
ISAIAH 53:6

To elaborate a little on the characteristics of human nature, here is another biblical glimpse:

For rebellion is as the sin of witchcraft, And stubbornness
is as iniquity and idolatry.
1 SAMUEL 15:23

Expect Resistance To Training

"I won't." Who has not responded this way? It is as though you were bewitched. In this mood, it is as though you idolized your own ideas and were ready to take on the whole establishment.

> *"Limits reveal the spirit. They do not cause it."*

Limits reveal the spirit. They do not cause it.

It is normal and natural to want to do things the way you want to do them. A child is persistent in wanting to do what he wants to do.

Adults are the same way. How long must you supervise people in a business? As long as you have your business open. As long as they are your responsibility.

This is no problem to you if you accept the fact of resistance and accept the responsibility for dealing with it.

God's Word does not teach us to fulfill the desires of our children. God says to train them in the way that they should go. God does not imply that they will welcome your training. The fact is, they may stubbornly disagree with you every step of the way. Remember, you are the trainer; they are the trainees. As such they do not decide the rules; they follow them!

> *God's Word does not teach us to fulfill the desires of our children. God says to train them in the way that they should go.*

And what if they do not? Then you help them until they do.

This is a positive approach to parenthood.

We train, we provide an example, and we correct; it is our responsibility. State why you agree or disagree.

_____

_____

_____

_____

Parents need to keep firmly in mind that they are the trainers. As such they are to provide knowledge, supervision, help, determination, standards, and whatever pressure is necessary to accomplish their goals.

If you think your children will be delighted with everything you want them to do, you have an expectation that is unrealistic. If you intend to keep your children smiling all day long, you are tackling a futile venture. If you consider yourself a failure because your children dislike what you want them to do at times, you misunderstand the nature of your children. They want their own way. You can expect resistance.

> *"If you think your children will be delighted with everything you want them to do, you have an expectation that is unrealistic."*

Once a lady asked me, "How do you get your children to do what you want them to do without getting angry at them?"

She had a teenage daughter whose job was to empty out the dishwasher. Her mother would call out, "The dishes are ready," in a nice voice. (No child.) She would call out again.

"The dishes are ready." (Nothing happened.) Then, "The dishes are READY!" Still no movement.

"DID you hear me? (Now at a shout.) The DISHES are READY!" (Still no child.)

132

By then, the mother told me, "I'm so mad I wipe my hands on my apron and go into the living room screaming, "YOU GET OUT THERE AND TAKE CARE OF THOSE DISHES!!"

Then she does it. How do you get her to do it without getting so mad at her first?

What advice would you give this parent?

I said, "Lady, do me a favor. Tomorrow night, when the dishes are ready, you call out just as nice as you know how, 'The dishes are ready' and then go after her." She did.

What a surprised child her daughter was. Imagine mother meaning what she says when she is in a good mood! What had happened here was that the little girl had discovered her mother was not serious until she was fighting mad. She did not need to pay attention to her until then. This mother had a normal, natural problem— dealing with the resistance of her child to certain limits, and dealing with her own response to the child's resistance. The simple solution was to enforce her first friendly call rather than her fourth angry call. This lady was teaching her daughter the art of non-compliance.

"Dad, You Should Take Better Care..."

Obviously, your children will not resist all limits. We had no problem with our son over his job of keeping the car clean. He wanted to keep the car clean. In fact, he was on my back, "Dad, you should take better care of the car."

If you understand the nature of resistance, you will simply accept the responsibility for helping your children. One lady asked me, "How do I get my daughter to stay home? I say to my daughter, 'I do not want you to go out tonight,' and she walks past me and out she goes. You just can't do anything with children these days. They won't listen to you. What do you do?"

> "If we understand the nature of resistance, we will simply accept the responsibility for helping our children."

The solution is simple. Get between her and the door. You need to help her stay home. You do not expect her to jump up and down with glee. Your responsibility is to guide her in the way she should go. Your judgment will not necessarily be accepted by your child.

APPLICATION (OBEDIENCE TO GOD)

What did God teach me today:

_____

_____

Applying what God is pointing out to you is essential. How will you obey the Lord today?

_____

_____

Write a short prayer to God that summarizes your thoughts.

_____

_____

What are you going to do, say, or think today that will demonstrate obedience to God?

_____

_____

THOUGHT FOR THE DAY
Resistance is the essence of human nature.

DAY 2—REASONS DO NOT OVERCOME RESISTANCE

Wouldn't it be great if your children would simply obey after you explained to them why you wanted them to do what you ask?

Have you ever tried to explain to a child why it is in his best interests to stay home when he insists on going out? What happened?

_____

_____

_____

_____

Children could care less about your reasons when they do not want to do something. The smarter they are, the more ingenious they will be in trying to do what they want to do. At this point they do not want your attention. They want their own way and will do anything to get it.

What do they need? They need a good-humored mother who appreciates the contest and enjoys it. They need a good-humored father who is backing her up and who steps in to help.

My Mom

I can remember when I was a teenager attempting to talk my mother into letting me go out after she said I could not go. I approached her something like this, "Awe, come on, Mom, won't you please let me go out? Please, Mom?"

I tried to make myself look and sound as pathetic as possible, appealing to her sympathy and her motherly instinct. Surely she would concede to someone as pleading as I was.

What do you do with a child who is playing the martyr? One who tries to put on a sincere act and tries to cajole something out of you that is against the limits?

She said, "No."

"Please, Mom, please let me go out!"

She said, "No." I decided there was no use being decent. It was necessary for me to try something else.

"So you say you love me, huh? How could any mother who loved her child treat me the way you are treating me? Can I go?"

She said, "No."

"But, Mom, everyone else but me is going. You wouldn't want to make a freak out of me, would you? Can I go?"

Once more…the same answer.

What else could I think of? You see, my objective was to get out of there. Anyway. Lie. Flatter. Whatever. But my best line was always the role of the victim. I figured my trump card was always, "So you call yourself a Christian. How could any Christian mother treat me like this? Can I go?"

> *"So you call yourself a Christian. How could any Christian mother treat me like this? Can I go?"*

She did not burst into self-defense. She had respect for my attempts to resist her plan. All she said was, "No."

That used to make me so angry! I used all the ingenuity and creativity I could come up with to make life miserable for my mother until I went to bed.

Sound familiar? When I was defeated, I would go to bed, thinking, "How does a fellow get saddled with a parent like that? Boy, if only I would die, then she'd be sorry."

I pictured myself in a coffin…my mother looking down at my dead body. In my imagination, I fired this thought off toward my grieving mother: "Serves you right!"

There was no point in appealing to Dad. He would just back Mom up. But in my better moments I was aware that they loved me. I sensed an attitude of approval and a real affection for me.

I grew up, was married, and had some children. To my amazement, I heard some of the same reasoning come out of the mouths of my own children. I found myself interfering with the wishes of my children. My children were saying the same things I said to my mother. The same things your children are saying…"Look what you are doing to me! A nice lady like you. Do you want to ruin my life?"

What your children want so fervently is not always what they need. You need to respect their wants. Their wants, according to your judgment, may not be in their best interests. The decision is up to you.

Affection

The Bible says it so simply:

> **Be kindly affectionate to one another with brotherly love,**
> **in honor giving preference to one another.**
> ROMANS 12:10

Dealing with resistance will reveal your spirit. It is better to back away from a rebellious child if you cannot deal with him affectionately. Take care of your own spirit first. Then come back and deal with the resistance.

A child's behavior does not determine your sense of success. Affectionate firmness backed by carefully thought out convictions and the backing of your partner does.

A Fighting Lightweight

I once observed raw human nature in the living room of a lovely home. A four-year-old was pounding a three-year-old over the head. No adult had heard what went on before the beating started, so no one knew what led up to the fight. At a time like this, you never find out who started the fight. It is almost impossible. So this is no time for a lecture or questioning. A swift rescue operation is called for. The mother did just that. She moved in without a word and hauled the four-year-old off his victim and took him into the kitchen.

"I hate you," he screamed at his mother. "Leave me alone."

Mother coolly replied: "I know you feel that way but until you cool off you cannot play with your sister, and I'll just wait here with you until you do."

This is where dealing with resistance all starts—affection—affection that portrays a tenderness, kindness, gentleness, and firmness no matter what the behavior.

By affection, I do not mean indulgence, letting children run wild, ruining things, or hitting each other. It is just that when you deal with children it must be done with a basic gentleness and firmness.

> "By affection, I do not mean indulgence, letting children run wild, ruining things, or hitting each other."

Sometimes neighbors must work together. In one case, a little neighbor girl was a biter. You can not order a small child to stop biting. She was playing in the backyard with the child next door. There was a blood-curdling scream and both mothers came running out of their houses. Sure enough. The neighbor girl had been bitten.

The children were fighting over the swing. The neighbor girl had tried to take over, and the child next door resisted. Biting is a powerful weapon and she used it. She knew she had done wrong.

One mother hurried to the bitten child to comfort her. The other mother hurried to the one who had done the biting and took her into the house. She said, "You forgot, didn't you?"

"Yeah, I did," the girl replied.

In this case the little girl was already sorry, and the mother's approach was much more effective than if she had glared at the child and said, "You little brat. I'll pound you for doing that."

The biting child's mother went on to remind her child that mothers are there to help. The storm was over. There is no simple solution to such a problem. It takes patience and closer watching by both mothers. In an hour, the children were playing in the sandbox with one of the mothers watching. In a year the problem had disappeared.

> "You can deal with your child's most obnoxious behavior in a gentle but firm way."

See what I mean? I am not suggesting that you let your children run wild. You can deal with your child's most obnoxious behavior in a gentle but firm way.

There is a difference between gentle firmness and hostile firmness. A basic affection for the child, no matter what the behavior, is an important building block to parental success.

APPLICATION (OBEDIENCE TO GOD)

What did God teach me today:

_____

_____

Applying what God is pointing out to you is essential. How will you obey the Lord today?

_____

_____

Write a short prayer to God that summarizes your thoughts.

_____

_____

What are you going to do, say, or think today that will demonstrate obedience to God?

_____

_____

THOUGHT FOR THE DAY
Reasons do not overcome resistance, affection does.

DAY 3—THE PROPER VIEW OF RESISTANCE

Resistance will take a number of directions. A child is purposeful about carrying out his own plans. Resistance might take the form of crying, temper tantrums, sloppiness, or pitting parents against each other with defiance and screaming.

This interplay between the ingenuity and intelligence of a child as it attempts to deal with parents is what makes parenthood interesting.

Respect

Respect implies knowledge about the characteristics and needs of the child. This is very important, especially with small children who lack coordination and ability. What can your child do and what can he not do? Often, a parent will be disgusted with a child because the parent is demanding more than the child can produce. To know enough about your child—to know what he can and cannot do requires constant attention, study, trial, and error. Pressures that work with one child may not work with another. For example, a quiet request may get one of your children started for bed, but produces a tantrum and resistance from another. Taking the second child by the hand or a pat on the bottom works better. Help means using whatever means will work to accomplish what is good for your child.

Admittedly, pressure is a force and must be used carefully. Because it can be misused, is no valid reason for not using pressure. It can be and will be effective if used by a friendly parent who is cooperating with his partner and has the best interests of the child in mind according to their combined judgment.

> *"Help means using whatever means will work to accomplish what is good for your child."*

Help In Accepting Limits

All children need help in accepting limits. A four-year-old girl is an example of this. Her mother, in despair, said, "I am rearing a little delinquent." This was true. The child was the terror of the block. Today this child is developing normally because her mother learned from a friendly neighbor the secret of setting reasonable limits and helping the child observe them. One day this little four-year-old was playing in the neighbor's house. She had scattered blocks all over the room. She decided that it was time to go home. The child went to the closet to get her coat. The neighbor said, in his firm way, "We should pick up the blocks before you go." "I'm not picking up any blocks," she responded. She proceeded to the closet.

How would you handle this situation?

_____

_____

_____

_____

This little girl needed someone to help her take care of the blocks. Realizing the child's need, the neighbor, gently but firmly, led her back to the center of the room. The child had no intention to pick up any blocks, and it was a real struggle for the neighbor to help her. With her hand in his, he picked up a block and put it away. He picked up the second one and the third one.

She said, "Leave me alone. I'll do it myself." He left her alone, but the minute he released her hand, she darted toward the closet. He went after her and brought her back. She was very rebellious and needed some more external help. She did not need a scolding or a threat or a spanking. Those techniques had been tried unsuccessfully by her mother. The neighbor started over again with the child's hand in his. She did not like it. She protested but they were getting the job done. He was not doing it for her. He was doing it with her. This is a very important principle. She was not just standing there watching him. Again she said, "Let me alone. I'll do it myself." He let her go. This time she stood there to watch him do it. He took her hand in his and started at the job again. Finally, the third time she said, "Let me alone." He let her alone, and she started doing it herself.

It is true that he did most of the work. It would have been easier for him to do it all himself, but this would not have taught the child what she needed to learn. He did not alienate that child; in fact, his house was her favorite spot for play. In his home there were definite boundaries, whereas she did not have the security of known limits in her own home. If she yelled, kicked, and screamed, the parents would adjust the limits they had set up in order to quiet her.

If a child screams in his rebellion, it is more important to see to it that he observes the limits than that his screaming be stopped. The primary issue should not be, "Stop your screaming." A child persists in screaming only when he gets the desired results. If your request is fair and reasonable, then with all kindness help your child fulfill it. You will not make an invalid out of him. You will be teaching him.

> *"A child persists in screaming only when he gets the desired results."*

"Train" Your Child

A father tells of an incident that arose with his very beautiful daughter. She was offered a contract to become a model. There was only one obstacle in the way. Her dad would have to falsify her age on the contract because she was too young. She came home very happy and enthusiastic about this opportunity. It would mean one hundred dollars a week for her while she was going to high school. Her mind was made up. However, because of his spiritual wisdom and personal integrity, her father refused to allow her to accept the contract. She argued, "Aren't you interested in my future?" She accused him of not loving her and not caring for her welfare. What was he to do? It was a very emotion-packed problem. There was a very simple solution though. It is not right to lie about her age. He might expect that his daughter would be somewhat less than delighted with his decision. A father cannot always expect his children to appreciate his position. However, he must do the right thing.

God does not teach us to humor the desires of our children. He does say,

"Train up a child in the way he should go..."
PROVERBS 22:6

God does not even imply that the child will appreciate your training. The child may stubbornly resist you every inch of the way. The parent must remember that he is doing the training. Because he is the trainer, he must have some concept of the goals toward which he is working. The day will probably come when the young woman who aspired to be a model will look back on this experience with her dad and say, "I'm glad he did it." That she may not be able to appreciate it now, he can understand. He should be kind and gentle and patient, but firm in his allegiance to what he knows to be right and best. She does not understand now but some day she will.

We have all gone through periods when we could not have what we wanted and could not understand why. Yet, when we look back through the telescope of the years, discipline and denial make sense. We need not be so concerned with our children's reaction to our discipline. The important thing is our wholesome reaction to their reaction.

> "We need not be so concerned with our children's reaction to our discipline. The important thing is our wholesome reaction to their reaction."

Do you agree or disagree with this statement? Why?

_____

_____

_____

_____

Express True Love

The mother of a young child asks, "What do you do with a child who deliberately disobeys?" For example, she tells the child not to eat crackers in the living room. The child takes the crackers and eats them in the living room. If she insists on the child's going back into the kitchen, the child begins to cry. The psychology books say you should be sure your children know you love them. How do you demonstrate your love? By giving in? This child discovered, that if, in her sweet little three-and-one-half-year-old style, she looked hurt and shed a tear her mother would take her up in her arms and say, "I love you. You can eat crackers in the living room." It is no wonder this girl is a neighborhood problem. Her mother says so and everybody agrees with her. What should her mother do? Firmly and gently march her out of the living room.

> "When your child questions your love, who is a better judge of your love, the little child or you?"

When your child questions your love, who is a better judge of your love, the little child or you? Sometimes a young child may blurt out the truth to a parent who is motivated by resentment and hatred. Then the parent needs to repent and seek to have the love of God restored in his/her heart. Then, whether the child pouts or screams, or throws herself on the floor, nothing will alter mother's genuine affection for her.

We are to "train up a child in the way he should go." This is a foundation block, a key in training children. All of our actions must issue from a wellspring of affection, tenderness, love, kindness, and long-suffering.

Maintain The Right Spirit

At a popular restaurant a sign posted at the entrance read, "No shoes, no service." A group without shoes approached the hostess, turned on all their youthful charm, and used all their persuasive power to get in without shoes. The hostess finally yielded. Did she do them a favor? A sign that says, "No shoes, no service" means nothing if not enforced. An un-enforced law is a farce. What did these youths learn? They found out that if you turn on enough charm, use plenty of persuasion, and apply the right kind of pressure, you can sometimes have what you want. They found that, for a time, there seems to be a way to get around the law.

Is it fair to the youth to allow them to lower the standard? Why?

_____

_____

_____

It is an unfortunate lesson for them to learn. When you get something you are not supposed to have, you do not enjoy it. Your own conscience judges that you have no right to it; nevertheless, it is natural to want to violate standards, to cross limits.

parent?

APPLICATION (OBEDIENCE TO GOD)

What did God teach me today:

_____

_____

Applying what God is pointing out to you is essential. How will you obey the Lord today?

_____

_____

Write a short prayer to God that summarizes your thoughts.

_____

_____

What are you going to do, say, or think today that will demonstrate obedience to God?

_____

_____

THOUGHT FOR THE DAY
A parent must remember, he/she is the
trainer, not the child.

DAY 4—SIN IS THE ROOT OF RESISTANCE

The Bible tells us that

...all have sinned and fall short of the glory of God.
ROMANS 3:23

What is sin? This is a word that many people dislike. Sin is selfishness. This includes bitterness, stubbornness, rebellion, anger, wrath, malice, hostility, and disobedience to parents. As we look upon our tender little ones, they seem clean and pure and innocent. We wish children were as innocent as they look, but we know that in their hearts lie the potential for all kinds of sin. They will sulk, pout, throw tantrums, cry, and argue.

Children Are Sinners

No one has yet presented the problem of a child who never disobeys. Did you ever hear of a child like that? To rebel is normal. It is part of human nature. Every time you give birth to a child, he will be disobedient by nature. You may not like this, and the fact may make you feel uncomfortable. You wish it were not true, and many cannot believe it is. Both the Bible and experience, however, tell us that it is true. When you set a limit, your child will tend to want to break it. This is as normal as breathing. This applies not only to children. All of us have the tendency to rebellion.

> *"When you set a limit, your child will tend to want to break it."*

One of the biggest battles in counseling with tense, anxious, frustrated Christians is that of convincing them that they have sinned. "Are we not finished with sin when we are saved?" they ask. What is it that causes two Christians to have violent differences? It is sin (1 Corinthians 3:3). Transgression of the law in any detail is sin. The Bible tells us:

For whoever shall keep the whole law, and yet stumble
in one point, he is guilty of all.
JAMES 2:10

If we could only realize the subtlety of sin! If only as Christian adults we could grasp the truth that when we have said or felt or thought or desired something that is out of line with the revealed will of God, this is displeasing to God and is sin! If we would maintain a constant spirit of repentance, we could save ourselves the frustrations of many a tense, anxious day and many a sleepless night. The next time you find yourself worked up or trying to control your tongue from saying something that you know is not right, be honest with yourself. Be honest with God. Get off by yourself in a quiet place and confess and repent.

> *If we would maintain a constant spirit of repentance, we could save ourselves the frustrations of many a tense, anxious day and many a sleepless night.*

Degrees Of Rebellion May Vary

In training children we find different degrees of rebellion. The first child may be easygoing. A second child may be a violent rebel. The third child may be a silent rebel. These are all different degrees of the manifestation of sin. Anyone who has two children will tell you how different one is from the other. You wonder how your training could produce such variations. Anyone who has three will tell you how

> *"Some of us can do wrong in the most gracious way."*

different each of them is from the other two! There is not necessarily anything wrong with you or your training. It is just that people are different, and we rebel in different ways and degrees. Some of us can do wrong in the most gracious way.

An example of gracious rebellion was observed in a nursery school. A little boy was there who had been told not to climb up on a table. He did so anyway. One of the women was about to scold him and take him down. He saw her coming, stretched out his arms, with a big smile wrapped his little arms around her, and before she could say anything, he said, "I'm sorry." She was about to say, "Get off the table!" Instead, she very gently put him down on the floor. She had no more than turned her back when he climbed on the table again. This child was just as rebellious as the child who might defiantly climb on the table.

Over and over, wherever there are children in this world, parents ask, "What am I going to do with my child? He won't listen!" Of course, he will not listen. A little child tends to do what he wants to do. Some children will be pleasant about it, and some will be objectionable about it. Either response manifests the same principle—man tends to rebel.

> *"What am I going to do with my child? He won't listen!" Of course, he will not listen."*

If you put two or more children together to play and leave them alone without any adult supervision, it will not be long before there is a conflict. Conflict among people in every age group is just as normal as breathing.

APPLICATION (OBEDIENCE TO GOD)

What did God teach me today:

_____

_____

Applying what God is pointing out to you is essential. How will you obey the Lord today?

_____

_____

Write a short prayer to God that summarizes your thoughts.

_____

_____

What are you going to do, say, or think today that will demonstrate obedience to God?

_____

_____

THOUGHT FOR THE DAY
Resistance reveals a parent or a child's sin nature.

DAY 5—THE CURE FOR RESISTANCE

You should be rearing your children with the consciousness that they need a Savior. They must find the power of God that will enable them to live right. You can control your children with stares, threats, promises, rewards, and many other techniques. The only effective control, however, is the child's being motivated by a love for God—not only by a love for you or a fear of you.

What are you currently and consciously doing to motivate your child to love God?

_____

_____

_____

_____

A mother, speaking of a son who had gotten into some trouble, said, "I am so glad he didn't tell me about these terrible things he did until I returned from my trip. It would have spoiled my vacation." She had told him that her happiness depended upon his behaving himself.

You must have a much better reason than this for asking your children to conform. If you use the threat of your own unhappiness, you deny the very essence of being and living as a Christian. And what is meant by that?

Just this: no matter how cantankerous your children are and no matter how upsetting the affairs of your life may be, your peace of mind in Christ should be independent of circumstances. Why do you agree or disagree with this thought?

_____

_____

_____

_____

You should teach your children these things, and they will learn them best by seeing a demonstration (Philippians 4:5-7). These are not just beautiful words. Peace, comfort, consolation, and joy should be your daily experience by faith in God through the Lord Jesus Christ. The resistance to your training should demonstrate these qualities in you.

Limits Amount To Responsibilities

When these are fulfilled adequately they form a basis for granting privileges.

Privileges should be deserved before being granted and should be withdrawn if the accompanying responsibilities are not fulfilled. For example, two girl friends, both fourteen, like to alternate weekends at each other's houses. This privilege is based on homework and duties around the house being completed.

If a privilege is no longer deserved, or if a request cannot be granted, the decisions should be made promptly and forthrightly. A child of any age can accept a negative answer much easier than a postponed answer. A decision, once made with consideration given to both the child's and the adult's point of view, should not be reversed unless some new facts are introduced.

Teenagers are inclined to regard certain privileges as their rights, like use of the car, choices of clothing, the hour to get home and to bed. It is up to the parent to have a clear understanding with the child about the use of the car, buying of clothing, and hours. Any failure to observe the limits should involve automatic curtailment of the privilege involved.

Parents should carefully avoid threats of punishment that cannot be enforced. Certainty of punishment is more important than the nature of the punishment. Empty threats encourage disrespect for the parents and for all authority.

> "Parents should carefully avoid threats of punishment that cannot be enforced."

One sixteen-year-old boy asked to take the car to the store a few blocks away. His father agreed on condition that he come right back. The boy came back an hour later, explaining that he had met some of the guys and got into a rap session. In this case a temporary limit had been imposed on his use of the car and he failed to meet the test. As a result he lost his driving privilege for a week. Similarly, a child who becomes reckless with the car should not be allowed to take the car alone until he becomes more responsible behind the wheel.

Your children will need help in accepting limits.

Take a question of limits involving teen-agers attending church. Parents ask, "Should you make a teen-ager go to church when he doesn't want to? If so, how do you go about making him accept this limit?" What advice would you give concerning this situation?

_____

_____

_____

_____

_____

What if my child does not want to attend church? The first issue is your own conviction—are you convinced of the value of church? Do you believe that to bring your children under the influence of a church is a positive, constructive thing to do? If you do, you should do whatever is necessary—whether he is eight or eighteen—to get him to church.

Of course, it would also be wise to find out why the child resists attending. Maybe by watching your life, he thinks church attendance is worthless. Perhaps you could give him some practical tips on how to get more out of a church service. Be realistic by admitting that you do not always seem to profit by every service, but that you believe firmly that a person can find strength, reassurance, and develop a relationship with God through being a part of the church.

If physical help is needed, your spirit should be one of love and firmness. Your motive is not, *you will do this because I said so*; but, you will do this because *it is a good thing to do*. Your child should realize clearly that you have a responsibility from God to train him in the way that he should go. Whether your children are teenagers or preschoolers, they will need your help in accepting limits.

> *"Whether your children are teenagers or preschoolers, they will need your help in accepting limits."*

For younger children you may have to demonstrate and make positive suggestions until they learn to use various limits and principles. One day three children decided to play a game. Each child wanted to be first. An argument led to pushing and pulling until Mother stepped in to help. She knelt down on their level and picked up the spinner. "Here," she said calmly, "let's let the spinner choose who will be first. Susan you spin it first; Freddie's is next; and then Tommy. Whoever gets the highest number will be first; the second highest will be second; the third highest will be last. Now isn't that an easy way to decide?" The children agreed and a simple suggestion from a friendly adult helped them get past a rough spot and enjoy the game.

Accepting limits will be easier if the parent enforces them firmly and with love. If you say, "Lunch is ready. Get washed and come to the table," be sure lunch is really ready so you will be free to help your children leave what they are doing, wash, and come directly to the table. It is up to you to enforce the limits you set up and to teach your children to carry them out. Failure to carry through on predetermined limits encourage disobedience and the idea that you do not really mean what you say.

A fact that comes up frequently when dealing with parents in the counseling room is that the limits in their home are not mutually agreeable to both the father and the mother.

> *"Much of the strain on modern adolescents results from uncertainty about which way to turn because the parents disagree."*

Naturally, when parents disagree in methods or outlook, the child is caught in between. Pleasing both parents at the same time is impossible.

Much of the strain on modern adolescents results from uncertainty about which way to turn because the parents disagree. The Apostle Paul wrote:

...fulfill my joy by being like-minded.
PHILIPPIANS 2:2

If we will turn to God, He will give us His Spirit of like-mindedness in the matter of limits, standards, and prohibitions.

Parents should keep in mind that their children will face limits all of their lives. At school, in church, and in the community there are limits or laws; do's and don'ts. The child who learns to accept reasonable limits at home can accept the limits placed upon him outside the home.

Uncertainty on the part of an adult about the direction that guidance should take indicates a lack of proper study and consideration. A sure sense of direction, so sure the adult conveys it to the child in word and deed, is essential to effective guidance. Look at the Biblical view:

> **The rod and reproof give wisdom, But a child left to himself,**
> **brings shame to his mother.**
> PROVERBS 29:15

> **Correct your son, and he will give you rest;**
> **Yes, he will give delight to your soul.**
> PROVERBS 29:17

> **As many as I love, I rebuke and chasten.**
> **Therefore be zealous and repent.**
> REVELATION 3:19

Adults who leave the child's achievements at the level of getting their own way and the child's development within the limits of their interest of the moment are not guiding. Such adult action or inaction is irresponsibility, not guidance.

The results of such an approach may be seen in the case of Beverly. This study shows the high cost to a girl when a parent lets her get her own way. Beverly had always gotten good grades in elementary school. "I can't do it!" she sobbed at my desk. "I hate school. I hate teachers!"

I learned Beverly was the youngest of four children, the "baby" of the family. Because of this she had managed to get her way in most things, and the habit had carried over into school.

In the sixth grade she had been chosen Scout treasurer after her mother put on a super feed for the troop. She was given the lead in the eighth-grade play because her mother engineered it. With other things it was the same. Mother could not stand to see her "baby" hurt.

But this year was different. Dad had been disabled by a heart attack, and Mom went to work. Now she had no time for a "buttering-up party" or to run interference for Beverly. Her mother could not run down the books needed for the term paper or coax a postponement of the deadline. Mom had laundry, house-cleaning, and shopping to do in the evenings and could not coach Beverly through homework.

In the past, Beverly had looked helpless, and Mom had sprung to her assistance. If looking helpless did not work, sulking and refusing to try always did. Now it was

149

different. Looking helpless got her an "F" in social studies, and sulking after school left her standing while the bus pulled out.

Mom had failed to guide Beverly in the way she ought to go. She had let her daughter have her own way. This was not child discipline or guidance, it was irresponsibility.

Of course, Beverly could not blame her mother for her childishness. I reminded her that Jesus said:

"In the world you will have tribulation..."
JOHN 16:33

The world would buffet her with schedules, demands, hard knocks, and even antagonism to her faith in Christ. But she did not have to fight the battle alone. "But take heart," Jesus had gone on to say, "I have overcome the world."

Beverly would have to grow up in a world that demanded maturity. To her this was a revelation; she had not known she was acting like a baby. No longer wanting to be a baby, she became a happy high-schooler.

Nevertheless, her mother had lacked the conviction necessary to discipline her, and lead her.

A child needs parents who possess a conviction strong enough to carry the child along, against the resistance or inertia. The decision on how to best satisfy the fundamental needs of a child rests not on the inexperience and inclination of a child, but on the parents' knowledge of the child's needs.

> *"The decision on how to best satisfy the fundamental needs of a child rests not on the inexperience and inclination of a child, but on the parents' knowledge of the child's needs."*

Just because a child cries for a candy bar, refuses milk, resists sleep, or insists on darting across the street, it does not follow that he knows better than the adults in his life what is good for him.

Mr. Main—had the problem of dealing with a teen-age son who would not go to bed when told. Because of the boy's late hours, his school work suffered and eventually he contracted an illness. An important cause, the doctor reported, was fatigue. This boy's parents had failed him.

What makes a child thrive physically and socially are adult-decided responsibilities which are gradually given over to the child as he shows himself capable of handling decisions and responsibilities effectively. There is no magical formula on procedure. What you do and the way you do it is a compound of wisdom from God, values God taught you, and your inner strengths.

Points To Ponder

When you must do something about an incident involving your child, you need to remember some specific helps as you approach him in a positive manner.

1. Physical and Verbal Approach

When there is a disturbing incident among children, you must go to the scene in person. Such incidents are seldom a life-and-death matter. You need to arrive at the scene in a relaxed, casual manner. You can move rapidly without appearing hurried or upset. You seldom need to get there at top speed, with your hair flying and all out of breath.

Give thought to your first words. Even if the children are screaming and hitting, you can take a few seconds to consider what you will say or do when you get there. Tone of voice and choice of words are important. You can speak firmly, but in a kind way.

Get eye-to-eye contact. It helps to be on the same level with the person to whom you are talking. You need not stand over your children, looking down on them and they up at you. Scoop them up in your arms, or get down to where they are.

2. Attitudinal Approach

What led up to the situation? Often parents bear down on children with no plan of approach. If you are to be helpful, you need to know what happened. As you drew near the group in question, you may have seen the whole situation or you may not have. It is equally important that you know what was said between the children. Parents tend to ignore the words exchanged between children. If you do not know what happened, your first task is not to say, "You kids, quit your fighting!" No doubt they want to quit as much as you want them to quit. Rather, your first task is to find out what led up to the situation. This need not be a cross-examination. If everyone talks to you at once, or if there is disagreement over what happened, you simply will not get the facts.

Remedy the situation. You will need to take action with or without the facts. If you can get the facts easily, you will be fortunate. If you lack information, be aware of your lack. Perhaps the children were too loosely supervised in the first place. There was no one around to see what was happening until the outburst occurred. Be slow to judge or to fix blame. Keep your questions to a minimum. Remember that your firm, kind manner will be the key to the situation. Never give a choice unless you are prepared to accept either choice. The children may need help through positive, firm adult action. You can try distraction, channeling their activities in another direction, isolation, retiring disputed equipment, or kind physical restraint.

Trial and error on the part of the adults are involved. Your first attempt may or may not be successful. No one makes perfect decisions always. The final result may not mean happiness for all concerned. You may need to help a child accept frustration. This is often done best in silence. To illustrate, your child might tearfully sob, "I want that truck." But he cannot have the truck just now. Within you, silent acceptance and sympathy for his desire are in order. This is no time for a lecture on sharing. This is the time for a demonstration.

You need to accept children's negative reactions in a tense moment, but you need not give in to them. Remember that, in the perspective of a year of living, this is just an incident and that you are the steadying, dependable influence. You never know what your children will do next, but they ought to know what you will do next. When the incident is over, cease talking about it.

APPLICATION (OBEDIENCE TO GOD)

What did God teach me today:

_____

_____

Applying what God is pointing out to you is essential. How will you obey the Lord today?

_____

_____

Write a short prayer to God that summarizes your thoughts.

_____

_____

What are you going to do, say, or think today that will demonstrate obedience to God?

_____

_____

THOUGHT FOR THE DAY
The cure for resistance is teaching your child to love God.

UNIT 10

SUPERVISION

THOUGHT STARTER

Supervision involves setting limits, dealing with resistance, and giving help.

MEMORY VERSE

**My son, keep your father's command...When you roam, they will
lead you; When you sleep, they will keep you;
And when you awake, they will speak with you.**
PROVERBS 6:20, 22

DAY 1—FAMILY DEVELOPMENT

Setting limits...dealing with resistance...giving help. Put them together and give them one name. That name would be supervision.

A Championship Coach

Supervision should be considered a positive activity. Let me tell you about my basketball coach.

We had a championship team one year because we had a championship coach. All of us on the team regarded him with admiration, affection, and good will. Occasionally, we dreaded him.

For me, it was when he watched me practice. A player wants to look good when the coach is watching. My thought whenever he was looking at me in practice was to get the ball and take a hook shot. This was the best part of my game.

Did that satisfy him? No. He always came up with the same dreaded sentence, "Good shot. Now let me watch you dribble."

Dribbling was the worst part of my game. If you were to describe me as a basketball player, you would say my footwork was good, my teamwork was good, my passing was good, and my shooting was good. But what did the coach concentrate on? My dribbling!

It was not as though he did not know about my abilities. He agreed I was a good basketball player. One must be to play on a championship team.

He was a wise coach, quietly watching and firmly insisting on correcting the weak side of my game and developing the strong side. Before the year was up, I became a good dribbler.

To deal with the negative is positive.

> *"To deal with the negative is positive."*

What The Boss Inspects

There is a saying in the business world, "The employee will do what the boss inspects, not what he expects."

In the restaurant business, the job of the supervisor requires him to meet prearranged labor costs, food costs, standards of cleanliness, and more. This is not optional. This is his work–full time.

My coach had learned that a basketball player will do what the coach inspects, not what he expects.

> *"Parents, too, quickly learn that a child will do what a parent inspects, not what you expect."*

Parents, too will also learn quickly that a child will do what a parent inspects, not what you expect. Like the supervisor of a business, or the coach, a parent must be continuously and directly involved in making things happen. Some limits are easily achieved and require little attention. Others demand constant attention and effort.

You Gotta Believe!

There was a phrase that we introduced back in the first part of the book. It is "confident expectation." Supervision involves confident expectation.

Confident expectation assumes that you are doing something or requiring something you believe is worthwhile and in the best interest of your child. If so, you will have enough conviction to see it through, confidently expecting the child to appreciate your efforts in the long run.

In other words, you gotta believe in your plan!

People approach parenthood differently. Some seek to teach children what is right by punishing them when they do wrong. Others teach what is right by keeping the child in the paths of righteousness.

These two ways are represented by two common questions.

The first, "How should I discipline (or punish) my child when he misbehaves?" The thought behind the question is that a child will behave if he is made to suffer if he misbehaves.

To illustrate this approach, one parent wanted to teach her child not to spill her milk. Her approach was this, "If you spill your milk, I will spank you."

She looked on as the child proceeded to spill her milk and then spanked her. This process was repeated for many weeks. The pattern of teaching between this mother and child became, "If you do it, or refuse to do it, I will hit you."

The second question, "How can I discipline (or guide) my child into paths of righteousness?"

Another parent wanted to teach her child not to spill her milk. She watched closely, teaching the child to put the glass down far enough out of range so that random movements would not spill the milk.

"Put the glass over here so you won't spill your milk." When the child forgot, her mother reminded her. At times, the child chose to defy her mother and deliberately sought to spill the milk. The mother, moving quickly, simply prevented the child from doing it. Sometimes she spanked the child's hand to teach her that she would not be allowed to spill the milk. The pattern of teaching between mother and child became, "This is what we do. I will see that you do it."

> *The pattern of teaching between mother and child became, "This is what we do. I will see that you do it."*

Both parents had to deal with defiance. Both sought to accomplish the same thing. However, there were two distinct approaches. In one case, allowing a child to disobey and then punishing her; in the other, teaching a child what to do and using whatever means necessary to see that the child did it.

This second purpose more nearly fulfills the familiar Bible verse:

Train up a child in the way he should go, And when he is old he will not depart from it.
PROVERBS 22:6

The secret of discipline is the setting of reasonable limits and enforcing them consistently in kindness. If you say, "It is bedtime," lay down your newspaper and in a kind but firm manner, help your child do what you want him to do.

> *"The secret of discipline is the setting of reasonable limits and enforcing them consistently in kindness."*

APPLICATION (OBEDIENCE TO GOD)

What did God teach me today:

_____

_____

Applying what God is pointing out to you is essential. How will you obey the Lord today?

_____

_____

Write a short prayer to God that summarizes your thoughts.

_____

_____

What are you going to do, say, or think today that will demonstrate obedience to God?

_____

_____

THOUGHT FOR THE DAY
Set reasonable limits and enforce them consistently.

DAY 2—POSITIVE APPROACH IN SUPERVISION

Many times in a day your child will need your help with dressing, eating, playing, carrying out a task, or obeying a limit. You will need to be continually redirecting an activity, resolving a conflict with another child, and the like. Many times in a day, an adult decision followed by appropriate action is necessary.

A little boy four years of age was in an ugly mood. He was looking for trouble. When his playmate came along, he knocked him down and was pounding him. His mother pulled him off. He was kicking, screaming, and yelling as she marched him into the house. He hissed, "Let me alone. I'm going to cut you up in pieces and throw you in the garbage can!"

Mother replied, "I know you feel that way, but until you cool off you cannot be out there with the rest of the children. I'll just wait here with you until you do."

She did not react negatively to his negative behavior. She was firm with him, and isolated him until he cooled off. This is what is meant by a positive approach. We can, by God's grace, maintain a spirit of tenderness, kindness, and gentleness regardless of the child's behavior. Parents need not look at every incident that happens during the day as a crisis, but as part of a continuing learning process. Parents must remember that they are teachers. Accordingly, any incident should be viewed in the perspective of years of learning.

"Parents need not look at every incident that happens during the day as a crisis, but as part of a continuing learning process."

Do you see the underlying principle here? It is not suggested that you let your children run wild. That must be emphasized. You can deal with your child's most obnoxious behavior in a gentle but firm way. There is a difference between gentle firmness and hostile firmness. A basic tenderness for the child, no matter what the behavior at the moment, is an important invisible help in training children.

There is a difference between gentle firmness and hostile firmness.

The key to the situation was the manner of the adults involved. Kindly and firmly insisting that children behave is far more effective than indulging them, letting them run wild, or allowing them their every whim.

The key to a positive approach is an over-all kind feeling for children, not a reaction to what they do at the moment. It takes many years for a child to become an adult. Parents need to be consistent.

Weekend At The Lake

Supervision begins with an adult decision. One time we met a family at a conference in Wisconsin. Since they were returning from the conference to Toronto and would travel near our summer cabin on Lake Michigan, we invited them to spend a few days with our family.

> *"Supervision begins with an adult decision."*

We extended the invitation without realizing what turmoil it would cause the family. The problem was this—the family was traveling to Toronto, where the grandparents of the two children lived. The children could not seem to wait to get back with grandpa and grandma.

Then along we came with our invitation. So the dad announced, "We're going to stop at the Brandts on the way."

It is a very scenic spot. It has all kinds of facilities. Good food. Great view of a big lake. Sunshine. Games. All of this made a happy combination between camping out and comfort.

You would expect cheers, right? Well, that is not what echoed through the car when the announcement was made.

"You never heard such a hue and cry," the dad recounted to me. "They wanted to go to grandpa and grandma's right now. And that was that."

How would you handle the children's complaint?

_____

_____

_____

Wisely, the mom and dad did not make a big issue out of it. There were no big arguments, no yelling to the kids to stop their protesting. No big confrontation. Just, "Well, we're going to do it. And I think you'll really enjoy it."

When the family pulled up to the beautiful lake-shore cabin, the children were resentful and skeptical about the events of the next two days. The following Monday you could hardly drag the kids away—even though it was time to leave for their grandparents' house.

The parents' plan formed a foundation for supervision. Knowing the children and the fun awaiting them,they stuck to the plan with the confident expectation that the children would benefit.

From Sandbox To Curfew

Supervision assures staying within boundaries. A lady put her toddler in a sandbox with a little shovel and went into the house. The mother said, "Now, you stay there till I come back."

> *"Supervision assures staying within boundaries."*

A while later, she came back out, only to find the child digging in her flower bed. She discovered that she must either watch to make sure the child stayed in the sandbox or find a way to protect her flowers. Respect for flowers is too much to ask of a toddler.

One mother tacked a sheet of paper on the wall and said sweetly to her three-year-old, "This part of the wall is for you to color." She had read somewhere that this was the way to do it. She returned in a half hour and to her dismay found Ricky had torn down the paper and very seriously and busily was covering the wall with a preschooler's design. She learned a lesson at the expense of a new wallpapering job. What was the lesson? You cannot expect too much obedience from a small child without supervision.

> *"You cannot expect too much obedience from a small child without supervision."*

Reasoning is not effective as a substitute for supervision. Another mother learned this. As she tenderly put a coat on her six-year-old Ruthie, she explained carefully that the spring air was very crisp and this coat would give just the warmth to prevent a cold. Ruthie apparently accepted this explanation and mother went about her work happily. An hour later she caught a glimpse of Ruthie playing in a flimsy blouse. The coat was on the grass, soaking up the spring dampness. Ruthie had not absorbed her mother's concern over her health. It simply got too hot with the coat on. The result? A cold that lasted for days.

Whose responsibility was it? The child disobeyed. But she thought getting too warm was cause enough for a change in mother's orders. Her mother learned she could not rely on reasoning about health over comfort with a six-year-old. Supervision was required.

The Girl And Her Snowsuit

I once was supervisor of some cooperative nursery schools where parents could learn about preschool children by assisting a professional staff. One day I visited the nursery school. It was winter time.

When children went outside to play, they were required to wear their snowsuits.

I came into the yard, and all the children but one were in the snowsuits. Where was her snowsuit? It was draped over the arm of the lady who was watching her.

"Why doesn't that child have her snowsuit on?" I asked the lady.

"She won't let me put it on her," the lady said. Now, think about that. Here is a grown lady buffaloed by a little child.

"Let me watch you try it," I suggested. The lady approached the girl in a frightened, gingerly manner and said, "Would you like to put your snowsuit on?"

"No," answered the little girl quickly.

"See?" said the lady as she turned to me. I asked for the snowsuit.

"Let me show you how to put it on." I took the snowsuit, caught the child, and as she was pulling away from me and resisting violently, I got one arm into a sleeve and the other arm in the other sleeve.

To my embarrassment I realized that is not how you put on snowsuits—but at least I was doing something. I was trying. I started over again and got one leg in and the other leg in, and finally—gasp—both arms. The child was tugging and fighting me every inch of the way. I zipped her up. The girl gave me one final dirty look and then suddenly ran off to play.

The teacher's aide looked at me as though I were a miracle man. What did I do? I did what I needed to do to help that child into her snowsuit. Did that child need a snowsuit? Yes. Did I do a bad thing? No. I did the child a favor.

I was just following up on a good limit—with the use of a little pressure.

APPLICATION (OBEDIENCE TO GOD)

What did God teach me today:

_____

_____

Applying what God is pointing out to you is essential. How will you obey the Lord today?

_____

_____

Write a short prayer to God that summarizes your thoughts.

_____

_____

What are you going to do, say, or think today that will demonstrate obedience to God?

_____

_____

THOUGHT FOR THE DAY
Supervision must be kind and firm.

DAY 3—SUPERVISION INVOLVES DEMONSTRATION

Suppose you are observing your children and some of their friends on the playground. One says, "Hey, I'm going to try out the slide."

Another says, "Hey, me, too!"

Just like that everyone discovers the slide and converges on it at once. They knock each other down and push some children to the back of the crowd. So you go over and pick out two or three of the children.

"Now, Wanda is going to go first. Then Mike will go next. After Mike is Joe." You line them up. You show them how to take turns.

So what happens the next time this phenomenon occurs? You guessed it. Everyone converges on the slide again—at once. Kids tumble everywhere. They trample on each other.

> *"Cooperation does not come naturally so children must learn as you demonstrate."*

You have to demonstrate again. And maybe again and again. Cooperation does not come naturally so children must learn as you demonstrate.

Too Much Time?

I can almost hear you saying, "You have got to be kidding! Do all that? Spend that much time?"

Well…yes. That is, if you want to put together that perfect play.

Look at the area of eating. When you first begin your child on the process of eating, she cannot even get her index finger and her thumb to coordinate. So you stick a bottle in her mouth. Or a spoonful of baby food. Next, you get her in a highchair and put a little food on her tray. You show the child how to eat the food and then watch what she does. If she throws the food all over the kitchen, you guide her hand to the food and back into her mouth. After doing that, you again let her experiment.

Little by little, you progress. Finally, she is interested in a spoon. So you help her spoon the food into her mouth. Then, you allow her to experiment with the spoon for a while. Even after she masters a spoon, it will be a while before she can handle a fork and a knife.

Keep the drama in perspective. It is an educational process. Each spill, each messed tablecloth, each soiled outfit is a part of that process. It takes a few years.

Supervision Requires Consistency

Supervision involves a lot of time. It involves staying with the job.

Roxanne was trying to teach her two sons to share. She started the process with a truck.

"Alfred has been playing with the truck. Now, it's your turn, Jerry."

Jerry started playing with the truck, and Roxanne left, feeling the sharing pattern was complete. She had hardly left the room when a cry broke out. Alfred had crowned Jerry and snatched back the truck.

Roxanne started the process all over again. She realized she had to stay closer and supervise the process longer this time. It took a lot of effort and constant watching to keep her two boys out of each other's hair. There was no such thing as a short cut. Sharing does not come naturally. Why? Because of human nature.

> **We have turned, every one, to his own way...**
> ISAIAH 53:6

This tendency is seen most clearly in small children. They will not hesitate to attack each other to get what is wanted. To expect them to share eagerly is too much to ask of small children.

When our children were small we had to make a choice. Would we raise grass or children in our backyard? We decided we would raise children instead of grass. We discovered that if you want children in your backyard, you will not have much competition from the neighbors. So the neighborhood children played in our backyard. We liked that, because we knew where our children were and we could keep an eye on them.

One day I was watching some children play in the backyard. Across the fence came this voice. There is one of the these, I suppose, in every neighborhood. It sounded something like this, "Laaaarrrrrr-e-e-e-e-e!"

Larry kept right on playing. The call came a second time. Then a third time. Everyone in the block could hear it. One of the children near him said, "Hey, Larry, don't you know your mother's calling you?"

"I don't need to go yet," Larry said. Then we heard a short, crisp voice, "Larry!"

Away he went. You see, his mother had two voices. He knew perfectly well that when his mother used that first voice she was not about to do anything about it, except make a lot of noise. She should have used her second voice the first time.

> *"Children learn to adjust to mother's screaming."*

Children learn to adjust to mother's screaming. Be consistent. It even helps save energy.

One of the most important helps I believe we gave our teenagers was to see that one of us was there when our children came home after being out at night.

They did not like it. But when your children realize you will be there when they come home, it is quite an encouragement to observe limits. They would often say, "Why are you always waiting for me? The answer was simple, "We love you. We are interested in you. We want to know what you have been doing, that's all. We want to make sure you got home when you said you would."

The older your children become, the more they need your personal supervision and the more they will resist it. I have seen teenagers get into trouble because their parents allowed them to have a party at their house and the parents took off, leaving them unsupervised. Your personal supervision removes temptations.

> *"The older your children become, the more they need your personal supervision and the more they will resist it."*

Reducing The Odds

In supervising, a parent follows up on limits. For example, a child asks her mother for permission to go out.

"Sure," Mom replies, "If you promise to be home at 10:00." The daughter agrees but does not show up on time.

"I wish you would listen to me," says the mother. "I want you to come home at 10:00."

"Yes, Mom. I just forgot."

"O.K. Now, next time come in at 10:00."

The child decides she has a 50-50 chance of getting away with it the next time. A 50-50 chance is worth gambling on. So the child tries it again and comes home a little later the next time.

This time, the parents are not even there. The child slips into the house and says, "Whew, I got away with that one."

The next time she goes out, she figures she has a 60-40 chance of getting away with staying out late. She comes in at 10:45. Mother gives her another lecture about coming home on time. Ultimately, the girl realizes that if she can just put up with the lecture every time, she can set her own time for coming in.

Better not to set a limit if you do not intend to enforce it.

> *"Better not to set a limit if you don't intend to enforce it."*

APPLICATION (OBEDIENCE TO GOD)

What did God teach me today:

_____

_____

Applying what God is pointing out to you is essential. How will you obey the Lord today?

_____

_____

Write a short prayer to God that summarizes your thoughts.

_____

_____

What are you going to do, say, or think today that will demonstrate obedience to God?

_____

_____

THOUGHT FOR THE DAY
Supervision requires taking time to demonstrate to the child the desired behavior.

DAY 4—SOMETIMES...PRESSURE

Sometimes, you must use pressure in your supervision. Children resist in all kinds of ways. For example, there is the question of church. What do we do about our children going to church?

My wife and I decided it was in the best interest of our children to go to church twice every Sunday and once every Wednesday. They had contrary opinions at times, but this was the considered judgment of my wife, the world's greatest expert on the subject of our children. It was also my opinion. The only question we had was how do we get them there?

Children have comments about church, such as, "Wait until I turn eighteen and I will never darken a church door again. You make me go to church and you will regret it."

We heard all the standard threats that you have heard or will hear. In our judgment (yes—in our plan), church is good for one, and the question of whether to go was debatable, but not negotiable. They could say anything they wanted.

One day, one of our children announced just before the midweek service, "I am not going."

How would you handle a teenager at this point?

_____

_____

_____

_____

So we had to help her get there. How do you do that? First, we helped her with her shoes. When a teenager does not want shoes on, it takes two of you to put them on. But between my wife and myself—and we worked hard at it—we put her shoes on.

The next step was to get her moving. We had to get her up but discovered her knees would not work. We worked at that problem for a while, solved it, only to find out she had a broom up her back.

Next, with my arm locked in hers she was walking stiff-legged, shouting, "I won't…I won't…I won't…I won't!"

It is difficult to get a person outside when her knees will not work and her back will not bend. It is especially difficult to get her into the car. But we got her in the car. We drove to the church and one of her girl friends was standing there on the curb. That girl friend had no idea how we got our daughter there. They immediately walked off, chatting happily together. All our daughter needed was a little help.

You ask, what did you do about it after that? We did not do anything about it. She needed some help, and we gave it to her. That was the end of it.

After church, she came up and said, "What do you say we stop and get an ice cream sundae on the way home?"

Well, why not? If I were to deprive her of one, I would deprive myself of one. I did not do anything wrong. Neither did she, really. She needed some persistent supervision with the confident expectation on our part that we were doing our daughter a favor.

"But won't you turn your children against church?" you ask.

It is strange that people will ask that question but they do not have the same sort of concern about school. Do you have any doubts about whether your children will reject school? When our children resist school, the only question is how to get them there. Do you have any doubt about whether or not your children should visit a doctor?

One of our children did not like doctors. When she needed medical attention I had to scoop her up, kicking

> *"Isn't it strange. People will ask that question but they don't have the same sort of concern about school."*

and screaming, plunk her in the car and drag her into the doctor's office and hold her down. There were occasions when the nurse sat on one end of that child, and I sat on the other, while the doctor let her have it with a needle. She was screaming.

Is that any way to treat a child? It certainly is. If I love my child, and that child needs medical attention, the only question in my mind is how to get her there—not should I!

None of our children has rejected doctors. None of our children has rejected education. They all went through college. None of them has rejected the church.

What Do You Do With A Charging Teenager?

A couple shared this experience one time. Their son decided he was going out. They had told him he was not going out. He said he was and headed for the door.

So what would you do in such a situation?

_____

_____

_____

The father got between him and the door.

The son decided to remove his father from the door. The son was almost as tall as his father and was in better shape. He needed a lot of help that night. A lot of supervision. They were both tired before the evening ended.

Will that shape the son's destiny forever after? I think it helped. What did it do? It proved that his father would do everything he could to make happen what he thought was best for him.

If doing your best to guide your children is the worst criticism a child has of his parents, that is not too bad. Your judgment might be a little faulty along the way, but there is no question about your intent or your effort. There is no question about your attitude or your dedication to your children's best interests.

> "If doing your best to guide your children is the worst criticism a child has of his parents, that is not too bad."

You must be convinced that what you are doing is in the best interest of your child. Confident expectation. Of course, you need to be kind, respectful, and affectionate—evidencing an attitude of approval...and be decent about it.

Occasionally pressure is necessary in supervision. Pressure is a force. The stronger the pressure, the greater the danger of misuse—and the need for mixing pressure with affection and patience.

APPLICATION (OBEDIENCE TO GOD)

What did God teach me today:

_____

_____

Applying what God is pointing out to you is essential. How will you obey the Lord today?

_____

_____

Write a short prayer to God that summarizes your thoughts.

_____

_____

What are you going to do, say, or think today that will demonstrate obedience to God?

_____

_____

THOUGHT FOR THE DAY
Sometimes supervision requires pressure.

DAY 5—SUPERVISION INVOLVES HELP[4]

Parents give help to their youngsters as a part of the thrust into life. The child is guided into discovering his own abilities and this guidance continues as he develops them until he becomes independent in his effective use of them. How can you help? He may need physical help for what he cannot do. He may need explanation or demonstration for what he does not know or understand. Or he may need encouragement, even insistence, for what he does not want to do or lacks confidence to try.

Before undertaking to influence a child you must be sure of what you expect of him. You must be sure that what you expect is within his ability. And you must be satisfied that it is worthy of both his effort and yours. Whether the experience you plan for the child measures up can be learned by applying three tests.

Think of a situation in which your child needs help. Answer the following questions for that situation.

- Will he find frequent use at his age and in his environment for the behavior I am trying to help him learn?
- Will he continue to find it useful as he grows older?
- Will it lead to other useful behavior?
- When you have decided that the goal you have selected for your child is worthy, another decision confronts you: Is this the proper time for him to attempt it, or would he learn with less strain and more profit at a later time?

These questions will help you decide:

- Is it simple and definite enough for him to know what is expected of him?
- Is it easy enough for him to learn without strain?
- Is it interesting enough for him to find satisfaction in it as he gains skill?

Most children, when they find the goal a worthy one and the undertaking within their abilities, will soon take over the parent's goal as their own and as they progress in achievement will require less and less help or encouragement from anyone.

A child may be guided indirectly or directly. Waring lists these examples of indirect guidance:

•Change the time or place for some of his behavior. (Give him his bath before supper so he can have a quiet story before he goes to bed.)

•Provide him with more or better equipment, supplies, and resources. (Fix low hooks for his clothes.)

•Plan situations in which he will be likely to choose, prepare and plan; take responsibility; or act in any other desired way.

She lists these as direct methods of guidance:

•Encourage his effort and approve his behavior. (When his wagon wheel gets stuck, you might say, "Good, you are lifting it out.")

•Give physical aid. (Push a little as he pulls.)

Help Involves Pressure

> "There are times when the natural inclination of a child is not in his best interests."

Guiding children involves dealing with resistance.

There are times when the natural inclination of a child is not in his best interests. There are benefits to him that you see which the child cannot see.

For example, a father knew that his teenage daughters wanted to learn water skiing. They were afraid to try. Knowing his daughters, he believed them perfectly capable of learning this skill. He insisted that they try and within an hour both were happily enjoying the sport.

Another child insisted on playing around deep water. He could not understand the danger. His mother scooped him up, kicking and screaming, and put him behind a fence where he would be safe. Ignoring his screaming, she confidently redirected his activity by getting him started playing with a toy truck.

This is pressure; it may be as strong or gentle as necessary.

In a restaurant recently, a preschool child was holding the door open, allowing a chilling blast of cold air to come in. The waitress talked to the boy to no avail. The mother said, "Darling, everyone is getting cold. Please close the door." He refused. The mother was helpless.

A man sitting near by decided he could help, so he walked up to the boy, took hold of his arm and marched him to his mother, saying firmly, "Leave the door closed."

The mother looked at the man admiringly and asked, "How did you do it. He won't listen to me."

The boy needed the guidance of an adult who felt strongly that it was a reasonable request that the door be closed. The child kept eyeing the man, but stayed in his seat.

Pressure is everything outside the individual that influences or directs him in what he does, thinks, or feels. This is a constructive force that slowly leads him to satisfactions he would not otherwise discover and to develop abilities he did not know he had. Pressure leads him to a knowledge of right and wrong.

> *"Pressure is everything outside the individual that influences or directs him in what he does, thinks or feels."*

Admittedly such guidance is a force, enough to overcome the child's resistance. The stronger the force, the greater is the danger of misuse, whether the misuse is deliberate or with the best of intent.

Many persons fear to use pressure, which prevents their using it effectively. Some parents feel this will incite hostility. Others fear social disapproval, that they will be thought of as harsh parents or teachers. Still others fear their own incompetence, their inability to carry through to success.

It is obvious that pressure can be misused. The parent may have his own comfort in mind or his own needs, not the common good of the family. Such coercion does incite hostility. Coercion dwarfs a child's development, never leaving him free to act or learn. To the extent that pressure is not resisted, it will make the child dependent for he has scant opportunity to achieve on his own and to make decisions from which he can learn.

Coercion used by the adult for personal gain is not guidance as we use the term. Guidance is the effort of the adult to influence the child toward experiences, which in his judgment will be for the child's development. This definition places squarely on the adult the responsibility to decide what is of value to the child.

APPLICATION (OBEDIENCE TO GOD)

What did God teach me today:

_____

_____

Applying what God is pointing out to you is essential. How will you obey the Lord today?

_____

_____

Write a short prayer to God that summarizes your thoughts.

_____

_____

What are you going to do, say, or think today that will demonstrate obedience to God?

_____

_____

THOUGHT FOR THE DAY
**Supervision requires pressure that leads
the child to know right from wrong.**

UNIT 11

THE TRUTH ABOUT CONSEQUENCES

THOUGHT STARTER
We do our children a great favor if we help them understand
there are consequences for their actions...good and bad.

MEMORY VERSE
**Do not be deceived, God is not mocked; For whatever
a man sows, that he will also reap.**
GALATIANS 6:7

DAY 1—WE REAP WHAT WE SOW

I have had distraught parents come to me and plead, "Please, Dr. Brandt, could you help us break up this romance between our daughter and her boyfriend? They have very little in common and are both immature. They insist on getting married."

If this were your friend's child, what Biblical principle would you use to help them?

_____

_____

_____

Then comes the same dreary answers to my questions. "How long have they been dating?"

"About ten months."

"If this match has been acceptable for ten months, what's wrong with it now?" I ask.

"It hasn't been acceptable, but we didn't want to upset our daughter or appear narrow-minded. We had hoped something would happen to break it up."

These parents are reaping consequences. They made a decision the opposite of their best judgment. Obviously, your children will marry someone they know. So you need to be careful who they know.

Another set of parents came in with their pregnant daughter.

"I told her she was seeing too much of that boy," wails the mother, "but she wouldn't listen."

"She would say, 'Mother, don't you trust me?' I wanted my daughter to know I trusted her, and look what happened."

What happened? The normal consequences of allowing a young couple too much unsupervised freedom.

"What can I do?" pleaded another mother. "My daughter parks in front of the house in a car with her boyfriend for an hour or two night after night. She refuses to come in."

> *"What happened? The normal consequences of allowing a young couple too much unsupervised freedom."*

"Why are you so suspicious, Mother?" she says, "You don't need to worry about us."

If you ask me, the parents should do something. There is a basis for concern. Her daughter surely is not reviewing Bible verses night after night for an hour or two out there. We all know what goes on in a parked car in the dark. But how do you get the daughter out of the car?

There is only one way that I know of. Help her out. How do you do that? You go outside, open the car door, reach in, and drag her out.

But won't that embarrass her? Yes, it will. This is the consequence of defying you. Won't she be angry? She will be furious. This is her problem.

What if she doesn't come home and parks somewhere else? Then do not allow her to go out. You may also need to deal with the boy and/or his parents.

Remember, this is your beloved daughter. But the ecstasy of physical closeness at her age is too tempting for her to handle. She needs your help. The boy needs his parents' help. The consequences of ignoring your parental responsibility at this time can be a poorly matched marriage, or, to say the least, allowing behavior that your child knows to be risky and degrading. The parents of teenage boys should know where their boys are and cooperate with the girls' parents.

At this stage, your children need your guidance and help the most. They will appreciate it five years later. Do not expect anything but resistance now.

When parents leave their children unsupervised, children will make foolish choices.

A Bad Break...Or?

In life you get some tough breaks and some good breaks. Either way, you take the consequences.

A young athlete grabbed all the football headlines in high school and went off on a scholarship to a university. There he did very well his first year. The consequences of that were praise, newspaper headlines, girls wanting to date him, and parties.

How did he react to his consequences? He reacted by not doing his schoolwork. The result—he became ineligible to play football.

He enjoyed the acclaim all right, but he did not like the consequences of his choice of not studying. He blamed other people for his choice. He tried to make his teachers out as being down on him, but the problem really was he did not study. So the consequences of that choice were that he disappeared from sight and dropped out of school, griping all the way about what a tough break he got. He became a bitter kid running away from reality. He was not ready to take the consequences of life...the good with the bad.

Another athlete had the same choices. He went to college to gain an education and play baseball. He made good grades and was a star on the baseball diamond with his outstanding ability. He concentrated on his studies first and was so good academically that he was encouraged to enroll in a dental school, which he did.

He was such a good player, however, that he was signed by a championship major league ball team. He became a star with the team, and he still kept at his dental school studies, attending in the off-season. After he retired from professional baseball, he had a career ahead of him in dentistry.

Two athletes. Both had the same choices. Both received the consequences of their choices. Both were rewarded.

APPLICATION (OBEDIENCE TO GOD)
What did God teach me today:

_____

_____

Applying what God is pointing out to you is essential. How will you obey the Lord today?

_____

_____

Write a short prayer to God that summarizes your thoughts.

_____

_____

What are you going to do, say, or think today that will demonstrate obedience to God?

_____

_____

THOUGHT FOR THE DAY
We reap what we sow...good or bad.

DAY 2—CONSEQUENCES..GOOD AND BAD

Our job as parents is to head our children in the right direction. To do that, we need to give some thought to the consequences that will help them along the way.

Some people call them rewards...or punishment.

I like to think of them all as consequences—good and bad. People make the choices and suffer or enjoy the consequences.

Adults know that the consequences of getting good grades are a better chance to get a job or enroll in college, and good grades usually result in more knowledge about life.

> *"People make the choices and suffer or enjoy the consequences."*

The consequences of learning to be cooperative are leadership positions, promotions, and raises. The consequences of poor grades and poor cooperation are trouble and missed chances, and difficulty in getting a job, difficulty in getting into school.

Such remote objectives as college, jobs, promotions, and raises are hardly of interest to children. But as adults, we know these are real. We know that our choices and experiences have their consequences. Even someone else's choices can affect us. For example, we all know of people who suffered terrible bodily injury and financial reverses because a drunk driver ran into their car.

I have a friend who lost his business because he guaranteed someone else's notes. The notes were defaulted, so the bank came after my friend.

There is not much point in lecturing our children about consequences they cannot understand, but we can teach them on their own level. It is a twenty year process.

If you do not study, you cannot go out to play. If you do not practice, you do not make the team.

> *"Announcing consequences and making them stick is one form of help."*

Announcing consequences and making them stick is one form of help. You force your child to study, and the reward is he gets to play outside. You make your boy practice, and the reward is he makes the team. You make your child come to the table, and the reward is he gets to eat.

If you allow your boy to use the car, and he brings it back in good shape, you can be lavish with your praise. If he does not bring it back in good shape—using too much gas or driving too far—he should suffer the consequences. He pays for the gas or maybe gives up his next turn to use the car. You are teaching him that his choices have consequences.

If your child goes out and goes where she said she would go and with whom, then you are lavish with your praise. If she does not go where she promised or come back when she said she would, there should be some consequence to face. She may need to pass up the next event at school.

Again, it is the learning experience, not the incident, that you capitalize on. If a child takes good care of his bike, he is entitled to your praise. If he does not, he must do so or he is grounded for a day. If a child eats her food and has good table manners, she enjoys the family fellowship and food. If not, she leaves the table or goes without dessert.

> *"It's the learning experience, not the incident, that you capitalize on."*

Suppose a child consistently refuses to eat at dinner time. Well, one way to handle him is through some judicial starvation. In other words, do not let him eat between meals. He will find that if he does not eat and is not allowed to eat between meals, the consequence is hunger.

> *"Suffering consequences helps a child get a proper picture of reality"*

Suffering consequences helps a child get a proper picture of reality.

Teach Consequences By Observing Others

There are other ways of teaching consequences. Do not let your child ruin his bike to learn a lesson. You can point out to your child how the neighbor boy ruined his bike because he did not take care of his.

"You know Sam always wants to borrow your bike. It's because he ruined his. You haven't."

Nor do you let a little toddler wander out into the street and get hit to learn the consequences. You can point out a dead animal beside the road and tell the child why it was killed.

A teenager cannot understand why you do not let him run around with undesirable friends. There are reasons. There is no sense letting a child learn the hard way on something like that which could lead to a pregnancy, trouble with the law, arrests, etc. But you can point out what happened in other children's lives.

One night there was a terrible crash down the street from our house. So we ran down to the corner, and saw two cars completely mangled and four young people equally broken. They had been playing chicken with the cars, seeing who would veer away first. They came to the corner and neither driver would give avoid the other.

My wife and I used that as a teaching situation. Here were young people who had access to a car and all the freedom they wanted. A half year later, one of them was still in the hospital.

There was a boy who could get his way by being cantankerous, uncooperative, and obnoxious. He applied his usual sullen techniques to his father when he became a teenager to get a fast car. His father was trying to make him cooperative and unselfish by buying him things.

The first week he wrapped the car around a pole at high speed and killed his buddy—the consequence of giving a hostile boy a fast car! We used that as a warning.

"If you're angry and hostile at the world, you can't use the car. You can't have it just because it's your turn. Around here, only friendly people get the car."

Losing the privilege of driving the car became one of the consequences of being angry. If you do not teach your children about consequences, they will have to learn when they are adults. So, we let them suffer or enjoy the consequences of their choices. We pointed out examples of other children's good or bad consequences. You can also supply your own consequences within your home life.

> *"If you don't teach your children about consequences, they will have to learn when they are adults."*

Here are some pertinent Bible verses:

And you, fathers, do not provoke your children to wrath, but bring them up in the training and admonition of the Lord.
EPHESIANS 6:4

My son, do not despise the chastening of the Lord, Nor detest His correction; For whom the Lord loves He corrects, Just as a father the son in whom he delights.
PROVERBS 3:11, 12

The rod and reproof give wisdom, But a child left to himself, brings shame to his mother.
PROVERBS 29:15

Correct your son, and he will give you rest; Yes, he will give delight to your soul.
PROVERBS 29:17

Because the sentence against an evil work is not executed speedily, therefore the heart of the sons of men is fully set in them to do evil.
ECCLESIASTES 8:11

There are some tough-sounding words in those verses: chastening, reproof, correction, sentencing, the rod.

Then there are comforting words: nurture and admonition of the Lord, love, delight, wisdom, and rest.

Here is an interesting mixture of words. This surely is not the picture of a mean, cruel, unkind adult venting his wrath on his children. On the contrary, here is a picture of someone familiar with the Word of God approaching a child whom he loves and delights. His objective is to teach and to guide.

APPLICATION (OBEDIENCE TO GOD)

What did God teach me today:

_____

_____

Applying what God is pointing out to you is essential. How will you obey the Lord today?

_____

_____

Write a short prayer to God that summarizes your thoughts.

_____

_____

What are you going to do, say, or think today that will demonstrate obedience to God?

_____

_____

THOUGHT FOR THE DAY
Suffering or observing consequences helps a child
get a proper picture of reality.

DAY 3—PHYSICAL PUNISHMENT?

When do I use physical punishment? That's the question you have been waiting for me to answer, is it not? This question must be viewed within the framework of the limits you have arranged. You are not to take your child by surprise. The limits should be clear. As I see it, the pressure you use should move from weak to strong:

1. If there is any doubt about a child's knowledge of the limits, then, of course, instruction is in order.

2. If there is deliberate dawdling or loafing, some reproof may work.

3. Taking a child by the hand and helping him pick it up, is still greater pressure.

4. Depriving a child of something meaningful may help.

5. Making something available that would reward a child may help.

6. Physical pain may help.

Examine your discipline. Do you go from weak to strong, or strong to weak?

_____

_____

_____

As I see it, physical pain should be reserved for a defiant, rebellious, conscious challenge of your leadership. It should settle the question of who is in charge.

In his book *Dare to Discipline*, Dr. Dobson says that nothing brings a parent and child closer together than for the mother or father to win decisively after being defiantly challenged. I agree. Nothing builds respect for you like confirming your leadership.

> "Nothing builds respect for you like confirming your leadership."

Dr. Dobson suggests a device for using minor pain for helping a child want to cooperate.

> There is a muscle, lying snugly against the base of the neck. Anatomy books list it as the trapezes muscle, and when firmly squeezed, it sends little messages to the brain saying, "This hurts; avoid recurrences at all costs." The pain is only temporary; it can cause no damage.[5]

A switch across the legs or a firm swat on the bottom will also help center their attention. How much pressure do you use? As little as possible, but enough to make happen what should happen.

Caution...pressure should be applied by friendly hands and used as often as necessary.

It is most important to be clear on this; if you love your children, you will chasten them. Parents chasten their children not because they lose their temper, but for the child's good—for his own personal development. Parents should discipline as they see the long look at the child's life. In the long run, the discipline will help the child be happy.

When our children were preschoolers, they taught me a lesson in the relationship of physical pain to chastening. I would lie on my back, put a child up on my feet, and boost him through the air to land on the couch. The children just loved it. This was a nightly ritual at our house. But one night one of the children missed the couch and came crashing to the floor. I thought the child would be injured. To my surprise, the child jumped up, eyes shining, and said, "Do it again, Daddy."

The other children added, "Do it to me, too."

I experimented a bit that night, and deliberately threw the children on the floor. They roughhoused with each other. I even slapped their hands.

They loved it and wanted more. A few days later, however, one of the children did something wrong. I grabbed the child's hand and spanked it with less force than several nights before. The child cried as if his heart would break.

What was the difference between several nights before and now? It was the emotional climate. A few nights before both of us were in a good mood and were having a good time. Now the mood was different. Physical pain does not necessarily mean punishment.

> Physical pain does not necessarily mean punishment.

Has your child ever come home proudly bearing a black eye? "I got it playing football!" Do you see how the emotional climate is important?

Some people think that if they never lay a hand on their child, they have not been cruel to them. Let's take a second look at this thinking. Most know about the pain of sharp words. You would not throw a brick at your child, but you might take a well-chosen sentence and let him have it. Sometimes a parent can hurt their child as much with a certain tone of voice as a spanking.

There are times in your home when no one says a word. No one is laying a hand on anyone else. There is just silence, quietness—you are being ignored, tuned out. Such silence can be more painful than if you were to strike your child.

Punishment and physical pain need not be related. You can pick up your little baby, as some people do, and kindly pat him on the bottom. You are saying, "I like you."

You walk up to a friend and slap him on the back, meaning, "I like you."

> Discipline and spanking need not imply a lack of love.

Discipline and spanking need not imply a lack of love. One of the reasons so many people abhor spanking is because they are angry when they do it.

The spirit in which punishment is given makes the difference. The use of physical punishment need not mean a lack of love. It just gets their attention. Avoiding the use of physical punishment does not always mean love.

Do you agree or disagree. Give your Biblical reason why?

_____

_____

_____

A cold shoulder can be just as painful as a slap. If you spank your child it must be done in a kindly, compassionate, tender way. Can you spank a child tenderly? Compassionately? You had better not spank him at all if you cannot.

The Lord disciplines and chastens you not because He lost His temper, but because He loves you. My concept of love is as it is described in 1 Corinthians 13. Love…

suffers long…is kind…does not envy…does not parade itself…is not puffed up…does not behave rudely…does not seek its own…is not provoked…thinks no evil…does not rejoice in iniquity, but rejoices in the truth. It always bears all things, believes all things, hopes all things, endures all things.

When you discipline your children, you should be doing it because they need it, not because you lost your temper. If you are out of control, do not blame the child. Get yourself under control before you approach a child.

These are important factors to remember as you develop consequences of your own to guide your children.

APPLICATION (OBEDIENCE TO GOD)

What did God teach me today:

_____

_____

Applying what God is pointing out to you is essential. How will you obey the Lord today?

_____

_____

Write a short prayer to God that summarizes your thoughts.

_____

_____

What are you going to do, say, or think today that will demonstrate obedience to God?

_____

_____

THOUGHT FOR THE DAY
Physical punishment need not imply a lack of love.

DAY 4—ATTITUDES

Attitude and viewpoint is important when a parent gets into this matter of making sure a child experiences the consequences—good or bad—of his actions.

I remember my team physician in high school. He had examined me many times and knew perfectly well that my physical condition was good.

Then, I developed a bad knee that swelled up so much that it filled my pantleg and hurt so much I could not straighten it. So I hobbled into his office with my sore knee.

Mind you, I was in good shape otherwise, and he knew it. Yet, he did not even mention my good physical condition. All he was interested in was my sore knee.

"Put it on this table and straighten it out."

Man, that was excruciating pain.

Next, he began to thump it. He wanted to find out where it hurt the worst. So he thumped the sorest spot a few more times just to make sure he had it located.

Then he smiled at me and said, "I have to lance it."

So he was humming to himself as he walked away. When he returns—with a knife in his hand—he was smiling. "This will hurt," he says.

Sure enough, he cut my knee open, lanced it and sewed it back up—all the time smiling, jovial. Then he said to me, obviously pleased with himself, "There—now you will get better."

At the time I was in horrible pain. I never had anything in my life that was sorer than that knee. Yet, the doctor was telling me that things were going to be all right. And smiling about it! My knee got better. Isn't it strange that a surgeon is one of the most respected and highly paid people in the community. We do not necessarily like what he does, but we like the results, even if pain is involved. He is not cruel, but compassionately helpful.

As in parenthood, it is not what you do. The results of what you do is the issue. Consequences should produce results in the future. Do not be afraid to see that your children get the consequences—good and bad—of their behavior.

The Mystery Of It All

There is a mystery to the entire process of working with your children. The matter of dealing with resistance. The matter of help. Respect. Supervision. Limits.

You must have a plan and then throw all you have into following that plan...making sure the consequences for a child's behavior are there.

Several years ago, a couple was having a real problem with their thirteen-year-old son. He was flunking at school, fighting with his teachers, sassing his parents, and fighting with his neighbors.

His parents tried everything. First, they ignored him. Then they praised him. Then they rewarded him. Then they reasoned with him. Lectured him. Withheld dessert. Took his bike away. Made him stay in the house. Spanked him.

Nothing seemed to work. But the parents kept after the boy—all with that attitude of respect for him and constantly showing real affection and approval of the boy himself. They also prayed for patience and grace. This went on for six months and nothing seemed to happen. Then, just as mysteriously as the behavior began, the boy began to change for the better.

Before, the boy had been condemned and censored by teachers, neighbors, and Sunday school teachers. Two years later, the same boy was a top student, on the football team, praised and admired by the coach, classmates, teachers, and neighbors.

This is the perfect picture of a dedicated, friendly set of parents seeking to train up a child in the way he should go. They realized it was a twenty-year process. Their concern was the process, not the decision of the moment. They had to hang loose and act by faith.

Trust Yourself

Often when parents talk about their children who are in trouble, I ask them what they should have done instead of just leaving their children to themselves. In nearly every case, if the parents had done what they thought they should have done, they would have done what I would have recommended.

Many parents do not have confidence in their own ability. They need to trust themselves. They need to go with God's Word, as their plan.

Any two dedicated parents who are running the family business as friendly parents walking in the Spirit have sense enough to make good judgments.

The main job: Train them up in the way they should go. You have twenty years to mellow and mature. By then your children will want to be like you.

As we said before...let's have fun.

APPLICATION (OBEDIENCE TO GOD)

What did God teach me today:

_____

_____

Applying what God is pointing out to you is essential. How will you obey the Lord today?

_____

_____

Write a short prayer to God that summarizes your thoughts.

_____

_____

What are you going to do, say, or think today that will demonstrate obedience to God?

_____

_____

THOUGHT FOR THE DAY
Attitude must come from a relationship with Christ, not a decision of the moment.

DAY 5—A BAKER'S DOZEN...FOR PARENTS

Hey, I Heard That One Before!

We hope that is what you will say as you read this chapter, for its time to look back at the last eleven chapters and remind ourselves of the principles in this book. As you reconsider these principles, consider them as more than just words—consider them as thirteen friends who can help make parenthood more enjoyable.

With a Little Help...From Thirteen Friends!

1. Confident expectation—based on the assumption that you are doing or requiring something you believe is worthwhile and in the best interests of your child. If you are, you will have enough conviction to see it through.

2. You need help from a source outside yourself—God Himself, through Jesus Christ. "If only my child would behave, then I would be happy."

The good news is that happiness comes from God, and neither people or circumstances can interfere.

But the fruit of the Spirit is love, joy peace, longsuffering, kindness, goodness, faithfulness, gentleness, self-control. Against such there is no law.
GALATIANS 5:22, 23

183

3. Parenthood is partnership. The basic job of parenthood is to design a harness both of you will wear.

Then make my joy complete by being like-minded, having the same love, being one in spirit and purpose. Do nothing out of selfish ambition or vain conceit, but in humility consider others better than yourselves.
PHILIPPIANS 2:2, 3

4. But the nature of human nature is to go your own way.

All we like sheep have gone astray; We have turned, every one, to his own way; And the Lord has laid on Him the iniquity of us all.
ISAIAH 53:6

In all our dealings, whether it involves your partner…or your children…or your best friend…the relationship will tend to strain at the point of decision making.

5. The husband is the president—and is responsible for making sure he and his wife wear the harness they both designed.

Submitting to one another in the fear of God. Wives, submit to your own husbands, as to the Lord.
EPHESIANS 5:21, 22

When decision making leads to a stalemate, the husband settles it. This is the key to it all.

6. The wife is the executive vice-president—and usually the leading expert on the home and family. In her role as such, she needs to have clear-cut responsibilities with appropriate authority.

7. Both parents must be effectively busy. Proverbs 31 describes the talents of a woman. It is a creative job to make sure both parents are using their talent in or out of the home. Jesus gives a formula for greatness:

"Whoever desires to become great among you shall be your servant."
MARK 10:43

8. Parenthood is a twenty-year process. It is a long haul. Longsuffering with joy is a fruit of the Spirit. You pull off a few perfect plays, but mostly it is daily effort and keeping at it for twenty years.

9. Setting limits is the parent's responsibility. The boundaries and rules (called limits in this book) are the result of adult decision, not a child's.

**Train up a child in the way he should go, And when he
is old he will not depart from it.**
PROVERBS 22:6

It is a family plan, one that keeps changing. Therefore, many meetings between parents are necessary to keep an up-to-date, reasonable plan.

10. Resistance to the plan is normal...so your children need your help. The nature of human nature is to go your own way. Children have a plan of their own, so resistance to your plan can be expected. They need a good-humored mother who appreciates the contest and enjoys it, and a good-humored father who backs her up and steps in to help. Here are some tools to help you overcome their resistance:
  a. Redirecting a child's behavior or attention.
  b. Giving physical help as needed.
  c. Giving more help than needed.
  d. Preparing in advance.
  e. Use pressure from weak to strong.
The use of these tools is a matter of making Spirit-controlled decisions.

11. Children need supervision in setting limits, dealing with resistance, and giving help. Put them together and give them a name. That name is supervision. It is commitment to the same limits and a personal involvement in making them work. Your style may differ, but the limits remain the same. You gotta believe in your plan!

12. The truth about consequences. Choices have their consequences...good or bad, comfortable or uncomfortable, painful or pleasant. Announcing the consequences for child's choices and making them happen is a crucial part of learning.

**Do not be deceived, God is not mocked; for
whatever a man sows, that he will also reap.**
GALATIANS 6:7

13. Trust your own instincts. I will put my hopes on the judgment of any parents who walk in the Spirit, respect one another and their children, and are committed to a mutually agreeable and mutually binding plan.

Conclusion
Parenthood is a full-time job. To qualify, you need to be a person of inner peace—the peace that passes understanding, given by God, and evidenced in the

unexpected, unprepared for, unwanted twists and turns of life. This inner peace, then, makes life a fascinating, pleasant journey, wherever it may lead.

Parenthood, to be successful, requires a partnership of two people dedicated to the task of blending their bodies, souls, and spirits into a unit that is dedicated to serving God and pleasing Him.

Parenthood requires an acceptance of the task, the desire to understand it, the willingness to be as diligent in preparation and performance as the most accomplished artist, businessperson, or professional person.

Conflicts and problems will arise. These can lead you to ever higher levels of accomplishment as God demonstrates His power through them. To identify problems and solve them is to find success. To cover them up or pretend they are not there is to taste defeat. Each partner should be ready and willing to see his part in any decision or task and do it as a dedicated servant of God.

> *"Building a happy family requires that you abide in Christ."*

There is nothing magical or accidental about living a life of happiness, peace, and joy. Building a happy family requires that you abide in Christ. There is nothing easy or automatic about it.

Guiding children implies a purpose and a goal. You need to know where you are going. You need to assume responsibility for influencing your children. Your influence for good or for ill will probably count more than any other in the lives of your children (Proverbs 22:8). You must work hard to make learning wholesome and effective for your children.

Parenthood is a twenty-year-long job. If you do your work well, you will lose your children. They will leave to attend to their own careers and families. Therefore, it is important that you should be effective partners, that you should keep in touch with each other and stay friends. You will reach your later years just as you started—only the two of you facing a new and glorious life together. You ought to train your family with this goal in mind—that when the day comes

> *"Parenthood is a twenty-year-long job. If you do your work well, you will lose your children."*

for you to say "Godspeed" to your children as they begin to plan for their own families, it will be a joyful day for both of you, with memories of happy years gone by. Then you can look ahead with keen anticipation because you have trained your child in the way he should go (Proverbs 22:6). Then you and your partner can look deep into each other's united souls and anticipate the time when the risen Lord will say to you, "Well done, thou good and faithful servant." Meanwhile, with mutual consent you can say, "Bring on our new life together and let us make it a fruitful one for the glory of God."

Let's Have A Ball!

The most consistent theme in this entire book is that parenthood can be fun. Parenthood should be a twenty-year adventure, not a twenty-year sentence.

Get that outside help from God, personalize those friendly principles into your life. And let's have some fun.

That's the way we are going to end this book—just having a little more fun!

---

[1]Adapted from Havighurst, Robert J., *Developmental Tasks & Educatiton,* ©1952, David McKay Company, New York, NY., second edition.

[2] *The American Heritage Dictionary,* (Houghton Mifflin, 1987), Microsoft Bookshelf 1992, s.v. "par•ent•ing."

[3] *The Concise Columbia Dictionary of Quotations,* (Columbia University Press, 1990), Microsoft Bookshelf 1992, s.v. "Children: Before I got married I had..."

[4] The material in this section is adapted from "Principles for Child Guidance," Cornell Extention Bull. 420, by Ethel B. Waring, Cornell Univ., Ithaca, N. Y., 1952.

[5] James Dobson, *Dare to Discipline* (Tyndale House: Wheaton, Illinois, 1971) pp. 35 and 38.

APPENDIX: SEX AND REPRODUCTION EDUCATION

THE FIRST TEN YEARS

Broadly speaking, during the first ten years of life your child is learning something about being a responsible person. The rest of the world divides up into broad categories—family, relatives, playmates, schoolmates, teachers, neighbors, men, women, clerks and strangers.

The tools we use to teach personal responsibility are familiar—respecting limits and boundaries, respecting authority, taking turns, rights of others, respecting others property, doing chores, doing homework, and accepting routines that are not optional, like fitting into the school, church, or team routines.

THE SECOND TEN YEARS

There will be some dramatic changes during the second ten years.

Read the following material as you think through teaching this to your child. Imagine that you are speaking to your child.

Body Changes

The pituitary gland begins to produce a chemical called a hormone. It causes the body to shoot up in height, and body proportions change. You becomes body-conscious (This is the time to teach the child about creation and the miracle of birth and growth).

Suddenly you are a head taller than your friend. You find yourself comparing your growth with that of your friends. It seems to you that all your friends are different from what they were last year. You remember that Jeanie looked like a bean pole; now she has curves. Art, who only last summer was a short, squatty fellow, has suddenly popped up at least six inches. Kenny has changed too; now he seems to be all feet! He's about as awkward as an elephant trying to eat peas with a knife.

Perhaps you are asking yourself, "What's going on? What's happening to my body? Why the sudden changes? Will I ever catch up with my friends? Or will they ever catch up with me? Am I normal? How come my younger sister is taller than I am? Why don't I grow as fast as Joe? Look how much faster I am growing than Mary. Look at these big feet, my crooked teeth, my nose and my weight!"

Various parts of the body grow unevenly. The arms and legs will grow faster than the trunk, giving a gangly appearance. One has the impression that many teenagers are all arms and legs. Facial proportions also undergo changes. Both boys and girls tend to grow first in height, then weight, then strength.

Teens differ much in the age of their growth spurt, and also in how great the spurt will be. Some are as young as nine or ten and others as old as sixteen before the

the spurt begins. For some it ends about age fourteen and for others not until they are seventeen or eighteen.

You will notice the changes in height, weight, and proportions of your friends. Perhaps you have been tagged with a nickname like "Shorty," "Tubby," "Slim," "Skinny," or "Shrimp." Sometimes teenagers can be very unkind with their teasing of one another.

One research study found that the average American boy at age 11 was about four-feet-ten inches tall and weighed about eighty-six pounds. By age 14, he is about five-feet-four inches tall and weighs around one-hundred-nineteen pounds. This is a gain of six inches in height and thirty-three pounds in weight in only three years.

Another study dramatized the great difference in height and weight during the growth spurt. Over a period of three and one- half years, some boys grew only 4 3/4 inches in height, while others grew 11 3/4 inches. During that period, weight gain varied from seven to sixty-five pounds.

The average American girl at age nine is about four feet, two and one-half inches tall and weighs about fifty-seven pounds. At age twelve, she will be about four feet nine inches tall and weigh about one hundred pounds. This is a gain of seven inches and forty-three pounds in weight in three years time.

It is good to remember that no one can hurry this process and you will be happier to avoid comparing your growth with that of your friends. Even if one of your friends suddenly is taller and heavier than you are, don't let it worry you. You are unique. You will grow at your own private schedule, set in motion by the Divine Designer.

You will end up so many feet and inches tall and you won't grow any taller; with a bone structure normal for you; body proportions—like chest and waistline measurements, facial features, head size, shoe size and hair color.

When you were given a name you could be easily recognized because of your God given body.

Sex Changes

The effect of the pituitary hormone on the sex glands causes the child to develop masculine and feminine sex characteristics. Your child becomes acutely aware of the opposite sex.

These changes are caused by the affect of the pituitary hormone on the sex glands. In men, these glands are called testicles. They produce their own chemical. Two things happen.

Male Sex Changes

First, bodily changes become apparent. You will notice hair starting to grow in the armpits, on the chest, the arms, the legs and above the penis. The voice box, called the larynx, enlarges, causing the voice to deepen. Your beard begins to grow. The shoulders broaden and you become more muscular.

Second, the testicles produce tiny cells called spermatozoa, or sperm for short. These cells make reproduction possible.

The seminal vesicles produce a white, milky fluid which carries the sperm out of the body if there is mating.

The day you notice fuzz on your chin, the time your voice changes, or the year you shoot up four to eight inches should be an occasion of rejoicing. Raise the roof, boy. You've just turned another corner toward manhood. You're leaving the boy behind.

When these changes come, you are capable of becoming a father at your age. What a responsibility. This fact should fill any young man with awe and a sense of stewardship and responsibility over his body.

Sperm develop in the testicles. They look like tadpoles, but are microscopic in size, about 1/500 of an inch long. In the testicles is a long tube, about 1/1000 of an inch in diameter and about 1000 feet long. The sperm are produced at the rate of 500,000 or more each week.

The testicles hang in a sac called the scrotum. A tube, called the vas deferens, leads from each testicle to a sac called a seminal vesicle, where the sperm are stored until they leave the body.

Here are some terms to know:

Penis—the male organ through which urine and sperm are released.

Testicles—male organs suspended in the scrotum. They produce the sperm and male sex hormones.

Scrotum—bag of skin containing the testicles, suspended beneath the penis and between the thighs.

Sperm—the male seed which fertilizes the female egg.

Semen—whitish fluid which contains the sperm.

Vas Deferens—long tube which carries sperm from testicles to seminal vesicles.

Seminal Vesicle—organ which produces semen and carries sperm to prostate.

Prostate Gland—organ which produces part of the material in the semen. It is surrounded by nerves which control erection of the penis.

Urethra—tube which carries semen from prostate to opening of the penis. It also carries urine from bladder to penis.

Females Change Too

Their sex glands are called ovaries. They produce their own chemical. Two things happen to girls also.

First bodily changes become apparent. You will notice hair starting to grow under the arms and in the genital area. The breasts begin to develop, the body becomes more curvaceous, and the hips broaden. Second, the ovaries produce ovum, commonly called eggs. The ovum is contained in a blister-like sac called a follicle. This sac moves toward the surface of the ovary and breaks. This releases the ovum into the abdomen, where it is caught by the hair-like endings of the fallopian tube and passes through the tube into the uterus. Each ovum is only about 1/200 inch in diameter.

When the follicle releases the ovum, it also releases a chemical called estrogen, which causes the uterus to develop a soft lining. The ovum moves through the tube slowly. If there has been mating, the sperm of the father have passed through the penis into the vagina of the mother. The sperm swim through the uterus and into the tube to meet the ovum. When a sperm meets the egg, they unite and a new life has begun. The fertilized ovum moves into the uterus, nestles into the soft lining that has developed in the uterus and begins to grow. This is how you began.

However, if the ovum has not been fertilized by a male sperm, it dissolves. The uterus will wait about ten days. If no fertilized ovum appears it will discard the lining through the opening of the uterus, through the vagina and outside the body. The discarding of the lining is called menstruation. From the time the ovary begins to produce sex hormones, this process of producing a lining in the uterus to receive a baby and discarding of it, if the ovum is not fertilized, will occur about once each month.

Menstruation is the mark of womanhood. Now that pregnancy is possible, stewardship of the body becomes especially important. What a responsibility God entrusts you with at your age—probably more responsibility than your parents would ever think of entrusting to you. This milestone in your life is one to anticipate happily. This is a part of being a woman.

The day you begin to menstruate is your graduation day! You have just passed a new frontier in your journey to womanhood. Life will never be the same. As your breasts fill in and your hips become rounded you can thank God that He has designed you to fulfill the thrilling role of being a woman.

Reproduction and all that it involves is a marvelous, amazing story. A positive attitude toward sexual maturity can be developed with the knowledge that this is a normal development, a part of God's creation to be carefully and reverently managed.

The ovaries are located between the hip bones on each side of the uterus, the organ in which the baby develops.

Here are some terms to know:

Ovaries—glands which produce eggs and sex hormones.

Uterus—the "womb" in which the baby grows during pregnancy. It is shaped like a pear.

Fallopian Tubes—tubes through which the egg goes on the way from ovary to uterus.

Vagina—a soft muscular passageway leading from the outside of the body to the uterus. It serves as the place of introducing the male sperm into the uterus and as the birth canal for delivery of the baby.

Follicle—blister-like sac that carries ovum to surface of ovary.

Ovum—tiny egg, released each month by the ovary.

Estrogen—chemical that causes a lining to develop in uterus in preparation for a baby.

YOU ARE A MIRACLE

Do you know how you got here? One day your mother discovered she was pregnant. You were tucked into the lining of her uterus.

Your mother's contribution to your life is a tiny speck called an ovum. It is so small that two million of them would not fill a thimble. Father's contribution is smaller yet. It is called a sperm, and a million of them could be packed on a pinhead. Within the ovum and the sperm, each contains 24 chromosomes. These pass on to you all the hereditary qualities of your mother and father, like family resemblance, a personality, intelligence, talent, and ability.

When a sperm and egg have united, the tiny nucleus is about 1/1000 of an inch in diameter. In order to get an idea of how big this is, cut out a period at the end of a sentence in a newspaper. Cut the period in half. Then cut the half in half. Then cut the quarter in half. What's left will give you an idea of how big you were when you got started. This nucleus grew hour by hour into millions of cells that form eyes, ears, brain, muscle, bone and flesh, all properly assembled to form a boy or a girl. At the end of the first month you were about the size of a grain of rice. Look at you now.

GOD CREATED YOU

The Bible tells us:

So God created man in His own image; in the image of God He created him; male and female He created them. Then God blessed them, and God said to them, "Be fruitful and multiply; fill the earth and subdue it..."
GENESIS 1:27

The human body is one of the greatest miracles in the universe—a creation of God. He planned that life would start through human mating—or sexual intercourse.

One of the greatest wonders of all is that the Creator would entrust us with the power to pass life on to someone else and add to this the challenge of training and raising the new life. What a responsibility!

There is nothing vulgar, cheap, or course in the kind of creation that makes such a miracle possible. There is nothing about this that we need to be ashamed of or hesitate to talk about. All of us—teenagers and parents—are stewards of life. If we view life in this way—that it is worthy of our stewardship—we lift it above the level of coarseness to a plane of respect, reverence, awe and even to being an instrument of God in the renewal of life.

THE MIRACLE OF GROWTH

When you were born you kept right on growing. You might have been treated wonderfully well or you might have had the worst treatment imaginable. But you kept on growing. You have had to make some choices that contributed to how well you grew. In fact, in the long run, how your body of is treated will be entirely in your hands. You grew on schedule. Not by your parents choice or your choice. The growth process was created by God.

Your body needs food, sleep, and exercise. Your mind can be trained through education. You must interact with your environment and you can interact with the God who created you.

You are a miracle. You are in charge of your body, whether you like it or not. You can alter body measurements somewhat by lifting weights, exercising, or by the food and drugs you allow. You can neglect your body or take good care of it. The same is true of your mind and soul.

If you pass on life to another person, their chance to grow and develop will in part, depend on how you managed your life.

MANAGING THE URGE TO MERGE

There is a growing attraction toward the opposite sex and a growing appreciation of the demands of society. These demands on a child give the opportunity to discuss five challenges:

1. **Getting used to an adult body.**
2. **Getting used to being a man or woman.**
3. **Handling new sensations.**
4. **Handling a growing awareness of the opposite sex.**
5. **Working out new patterns of living together with your parents.**

THE MIRACLE OF GENDER

The Bible says that God created male and female. If you have ever filled out an application blank you came across something like this:

Sex: ___**Male** ___**Female**

It never looks like this: **Sex:**   ___**Yes** ___**No**

At church and school you have suddenly discovered girls—or boys. Teen fellows will now be asking themselves, "Hey, where did she come from?" Come to think of it, she's the same girl you wouldn't have been caught dead with just a few years back. But now, she's different. And immensely more interesting! You have discovered that for some reason you find it enjoyable to look in her direction. As a matter of fact, you've noticed that she rather enjoys looking at you, too. Yes, girls have discovered that there are young men around, too. Let's take a look at how this interest in your own body, and the attraction to the opposite sex comes about and how it is all part of God's plan.

With this fact before us, we can give the boot to crude ideas that suggest our bodies should make us ashamed or embarrassed as we grow physically from youth to adulthood. Physical growth and change are part of the natural process of growing up; milestones along the way to becoming a man or a woman! So you might as well enjoy it. It's been happening to people for centuries.

WIDENING HORIZONS—NEW SENSATIONS

Beginning in the field of family life education early in my career, and looking at what is taught today, there is hardly any resemblance. What we taught then would seem like brand new, original material. I propose to do just that—*to present you with some very new, very old ideas.*

Since you have listened this far let me encourage you to give me a chance to propose a way for you to live a joyful, peaceful, loving life—beginning now and improving as the years go by. You will become gentler, kinder, more patient, more generous, and able to manage your urges so that they satisfy you and the people around you. Isn't that what you are looking for?

First, look at sex education the modern way. On TV, with a boy in first grade watching, there was a couple passionately French kissing, touching tongues. After a commercial advertising women's panties, the same couple were in bed wildly fondling each other. By the way, both of them were married to someone else. That made the scene much more exciting.

The message is that adultery is the way to go if your urges lead you that way.

On the news was the story of an eighteen-year-old girl who has AIDS. She was "sexually active." So far she has known six sex partners. Nothing wrong with that, is there? The wrong was a failure to use condoms. She could dispose of a fetus if she were pregnant with a simple abortion. Unfortunately, she can't dispose of AIDS. She is dying.

Then, on TV, there was a cartoon that showed how to use a condom properly. There were some TV ads for current morals that gave glimpses of killing with guns, vicious fist fights, blowing up buildings, and passionate kissing. It's enough to make you want to try it. When someone's behavior doesn't suit you, let them have it.

Of course, we are all familiar with the homosexual issue. Thirty years ago homosexual behavior was a psychiatric problem. Today, if you oppose such behavior, you are a psychiatric problem.

This is modern day sex education. Put self first, satisfy your urges, use people and then discard them, neglect your children, and ignore your partner. Sexual activity is as commonplace as going out to dinner. Children in diapers see sensual nudity regularly that people would be arrested for in a burlesque show 30 years ago.

The sad side of all this freedom is that it destroys good fellowship. A talk-show guest was being questioned why he was still single at 32 years of age. He said that he has participated in eleven weddings and not one of those couples are together today. For every two couples who appear at the marriage license bureau, one couple appears at the divorce court. Child abuse, wife beating, murder, and crime become more and more common.

People are restless, anxious, and frustrated.

Wouldn't it be nice if you could be kindly affectioned toward the people you must associate with? If you could have a sense of calm, comfortable, relaxed brotherly love toward everyone, would you go for it? Wouldn't it be nice if you could give anyone a place of being the honored one in your presence whether they deserve it or not? That is a possibility within your grasp. How do you find it? You earn it. I will show you how.

I am talking about sex education. I have in mind teaching someone who is beginning the second ten years of life how to treat men and women. In a twenty-four-hour day, you will spend very few of those hours in bed having sex. What I have in mind is how to relate to men and women the rest of the time.

Remember, we are talking about people who are created by the living God. He has a plan for us when it comes to managing new sensations and widening horizons. Compare this material to what you are seeing, and hearing, and reading today.

Paralleling the body changes and sex changes that give the teenager masculine or feminine sex characteristics is the experience of some new sensations. You discover that touching and caressing yourself is pleasant. Masturbation, or caressing of the reproduction organs is especially pleasurable. At the same time you learn that masturbation also brings with it some disturbing and guilty feelings. You discover some pleasant emotions for leaning against something like the bar of a bicycle or from wearing tight clothing.

GROWING AWARENESS OF OPPOSITE SEX

Teens soon discover that seeing and being near someone of the opposite sex results in a pleasurable reaction. This knowledge may come quite accidentally, perhaps as casually as a boy and girl sitting together in church. He entered from one side, she from another. They had not planned to sit side by side. Yet, they became pleasantly aware of each other's presence. There was a thrill in sharing the song book with her as his arm brushed hers.

You start listening in on conversations between teens at school, in church, and in the neighborhood. They describe the pleasure in holding hands, kissing, petting, and necking. Your curiosity is aroused. You may have experienced the thrill of your first kiss and will not soon forget the quick breathing, pounding of the heart, and the overall excitement that tingles in the blood. You discover reading material, pictures, and television programs that stir you. It's a new widening horizon that is opening up to you. These new sensations and temptations are difficult to manage, aren't they? When God gave you the responsibility of the stewardship of your body, your mind, and your conduct around other people, he gave you an adult-sized job to do.

PARENTS GET INVOLVED

A growing awareness of the opposite sex leads to increased contact with them and this involves your parents. Activities like dates, parties and outings involve their approval. So does use of the car, or use of the yard, recreation room, living room, or permission to go somewhere else. Parents are actively interested in your choice of friends and how involved you get with them. They want to know where you are going, what you are wearing, what you will be doing, and when you will be back. They know that this growing interest in the opposite sex can become a strong attraction that needs to be carefully managed.

A FRIENDLY APPROACH

You can drift into an attitude of resisting any interest that your parents have in your interest and fellowship with the opposite sex. They are concerned that dating will not just be a physical relationship which grows too rapidly, becomes too intimate too fast, and leads to marriage too soon.

It would make more sense to make an effort to team up with your parents. In a friendly, cooperative spirit, parents and teens together can examine the pathway that leads from birth to marriage. By so doing, both can see that the attraction for the opposite sex, the first date, first love, second love, and on to going steady and becoming engaged and finally married, are part of the normal scheme of development from youth to adulthood. And that this scheme of social progress has been going on since your first birthday! It is well to remember that the end result of this growing attraction for the opposite sex is marriage.

THE DATING LADDER

David Treat, the health educator of Flint, Michigan, has devised what he calls a dating ladder to depict the steps a child takes in his development from birth to marriage. Not all children will go through all these steps. In general, the infant, at first preoccupied with himself, will gradually recognize and respond to his mother. Later he will respond to his family, and more slowly come to include a wide circle of the community, including friends at school, church and wherever else he has contacts. You may recall having a fondness for someone of your own sex and age. You may intensely like someone of your own sex, but much older, like the Scoutmaster, a Sunday School teacher or a hero in the headlines. You may develop a crush on someone of the opposite sex, who is much older. This may be a national figure, a neighbor, or a teacher.

Soon there will be group activities involving both sexes. Church parties, weekend retreats, outings, hikes, and club activities provide such contacts. Then you will discover the opposite sex. Boys will view girls from a distance, talk about them, tease them, or push and shove them. This is the beginning of a process of pairing off, doubly perhaps at first, then single dating, going steady, and finally engagement and marriage. Ten years from now, nine out of ten of the teens who hear this will be married. Can you believe it? No wonder you are getting interested in the opposite sex. You will marry one of them!

MARRIAGE
Engagement
Steady
Singles
Doubles
Groups/Community
Neighbors
Relatives
Family
Mother
Self
BIRTH

WHAT KIND OF PERSON ARE YOU?

Have you wondered why your parents are so concerned about who your friends are? One reason is that you will marry one of them.

Remember that someone will marry you, too. Picking a marriage partner is only half the matter. The other half is for you to become a good marriage partner. What kind of person will the one get who marries you? Are you a happy, friendly, cooperative, helpful person at home? You do your work gladly and do it well. It is fun to have you around the house. If this describes you, then you will be the same way when you start your own home.

Are you crabby, nasty, lazy, or impolite at home? Do you do as little as possible around the house and do it reluctantly? If this describes you, then you will be the same when you start your own home.

The Bible tells you what kind of person you ought to be. Here are some examples:

"You shall love your neighbor as yourself."
MATTHEW 22:39

...whoever desires to become great among you, let him be your servant.
MATTHEW 20:26

"And whoever of you desires to be first shall be slave of all. For even the Son of Man did not come to be served, but to serve, and to give His life a ransom for many."
MARK 10:44, 45

**Be kindly affectionate to one another with brotherly love,
in honor giving preference to one another.**
ROMANS 12:10

Yes, your job right now is becoming the kind of person who is easy to live with—a mature, genuine, friendly, considerate, real person. This is important because it has a bearing on how you will act on your dates.

Dr. Popenoe has studied the subject of growing up into mature adults for years. Consider his challenge:

> "If (a boy) is to be responsible for his sexual conduct, he must have been made responsible for all other conduct in the past: for picking up his toys, handling his allowance, buying his clothes; for contributing to the welfare of his family in a democratic co-partnership; for contributing to the welfare of other families as a junior citizen."[1]

> This applies to girls too.

> "Dating is not a topic unrelated to the rest of life. The person who must immediately have what he wants, and have it without regard for anyone else, will approach dating and the opposite sex the same way. The person who is considerate, responsible, unselfish, will approach dating and the opposite sex the same way. It is easy to see, isn't it why it is important what kind of person you are and equally important what kind of people you chose to associate with? You will marry one of them."[2]

PUPPY LOVE

The natural attraction teens discover for the opposite sex normally leads to brief friendships known as "crushes," or here-today and gone-tomorrow relationships known as "puppy love."

There comes a new interest in grooming. A teenage boy will begin spending more time in front of the mirror, his hair will have to be just right, and he will be more particular about the clothes he wears to school. Why? He has met her. Or, he wants to meet her. This sudden interest in looking right and dressing properly is a milestone in growing up. A teenage daughter comes home with stars in her eyes, seems to be walking on air, and says, "Mother, I saw the most adorable boy today." She's boy-conscious. To her, the fellow she saw is the only boy in the world. Of course, she is only looking. Next week, or even tomorrow, it may be someone new. It is hard for her to understand why Mother is not impressed. It is because Mother gets accustomed to hearing about the new boy as the former one moves off stage.

DATING—WORKSHOP IN HUMAN RELATIONS

It is a short step from watching and talking about the opposite sex to dating them. Dating is like a laboratory where you get to know a variety of girls and boys. At the start, some teens feel awkward and self-conscious. There are new feelings and

---

[1] Popenoe, Paul, *Your Son at Seventeen*, American Institute of Family Relations, p. 5.

[2] Ibid.

sensations that are hard to handle. There is difficulty with carrying on conversations, getting dates, using the right manners, knowing what to expect of each other, and handling aggressive approaches.

Do not be surprised. The rest of the teens are in the same boat. Ease with the opposite sex comes with practice and experience. It is helpful to get involved with group activities first. This is one reason why churches have club activities like Royal Ambassadors, and Girls in Action. Here you get a chance to work closely with others of your own sex.

Special interest groups such as school band, journalism club, drama club, hobbies, and the like, will provide opportunities for contact with the opposite sex as well as adding an extra plus to everyday life. Participation in winter and summer sports will give teens hours of joyful entertainment. Skiing, skating, boating, surf boarding, tobogganing, fishing, hunting, and even such relatively inactive interests as bird watching and tree identification, can hold potential excitement and adventure for mentally and physically developing teens.

Appealing to many teens are the special competitive games such as basketball, baseball, tennis, and football. Others may be encouraged to develop musical skills.

Eventually, of course, you will pair off. Then the support of the gang is gone. You are on your own. You may struggle for something to say. For lack of something else to do, this is the time when you are tempted to "make out" or pet. You discover that this is really a very satisfying experience and you can easily fall into this pattern because you do not know what else to do and it is pleasant. But the intimacy is disturbing. You do not feel right about it. And a little caressing arouses passions within you—and in your date.

What is going on? It is important to understand what is involved. Both parents and thoughtful teens will realize the importance of friendly understanding "in the way that they should go" (Proverbs 22:6).

MAKING OUT

"What's wrong with making out?" is the question that young people keep asking me. The word we used in my day was "petting."

What do young people do when they "make out"? They tell me it is kissing, hugging, and caressing. The purpose is to fan passions that are pleasant and desirable; to arouse sexual desire. It is for the moment. Admiration and respect are secondary. It is considered to be a form of recreation. Should we go bowling, play Ping-Pong, or make out? It is an activity strictly for pleasure.

One young lady stated her problem very clearly when she asked, "What should I do? If I don't make out, the boy won't date me again. They say that all the girls do it. For a while I went steady with a fellow and we broke up because I refused to park and make out. He said all couples that go steady make out. I liked him. If you don't make out, you haven't got a chance."

The young lady is the spokesman for hosts of young people. She isn't quite right, however, in thinking that she is alone. Her question is shared by all girls who want to be decent and respectable. Boys who respect girls and want to please God with their lives must also grapple with the question.

Petting is intimacy and we are not strangers to experiencing and observing physical intimacies. From birth, children are held, cuddled, caressed, and kissed. We experience pleasure in picking up a baby and cuddling it. We enjoy touching the baby's warm, soft skin. Then there is the friendly handshake, the pat on the back, or walking together arm in arm. These are evidences of friendship and respect. People say, "We are close friends." There is deep enjoyment in being together and having heart-to-heart talks that share the deepest longings with each other.

There is also the embrace and the kiss of greeting. This is reserved for those who are closely related or who have a great deal in common.

Kissing and caressing are intimacies reserved for expressions of the deepest love, loyalty, and devotion.

The sexual relationship is reserved only for the man and woman who have married and pledged themselves to become one for life.

So there are many forms of intimacy. They all represent degrees of friendship, goodwill, affection, and respect.

We might as well face it. No matter how busy you keep yourself, or how interesting activities can be, you will sooner or later face the question "to make out or not to."

There is a problem here for all young people. Passion and desire is strong in both boys and girls. But there is a conflict. You know what is right, that physical contact implies respect, devotion, loyalty, and friendship. On the other hand, the thrill of kissing and the pleasant sensation of physical closeness is the highest of human pleasures. It is true that many of your friends are doing it.

Scores of pamphlets, articles, and books have been written on this subject. The teen who wants to please God will turn to the Bible to see what it says. Let's take a look:

Turn your back on the turbulent desires of youth and give your positive attention to goodness, faith, love and peace in company with all those who approach God in sincerity.
2 TIMOTHY 2:22 (PHILLIPS)

Keep thyself pure.
1 TIMOTHY 5:22 (PHILLIPS)

Do not then, allow sin to establish any power over your mortal bodies in making you give way to your lusts. Nor hand over your organs to be, as it were, weapons of evil for the devil's purposes. But, like men rescued from certain death, put yourselves in God's

hands weapons of good for His own purposes...You belong to the power which you choose to obey, whether you choose sin...or God"
ROMANS 6:12, 13, 16 (PHILLIPS)

Does this sound like some adults ganging up on teenagers and spoiling their fun? After reading what the Bible says the question still remains, "What can I do when the boy insists on making out?" Both the boy and the girl face the temptation of immediate gratification and pleasure. The boy's invitation has an attraction and a fascination to it.

What is temptation? A noted psychiatrist gives the answer.

Every day of your life, no matter how sheltered you are, you face some choice in which the wrong action is so seductive, so plausible, so pleasurable that it takes a conscious act of the will to reject it. Temptation is universal, as old as the Garden of Eden. Much of your happiness or unhappiness depends on your ability to handle it—instead of letting it handle you.[3]

Take the case of Barb. Petting led her into a dangerous, heartbreaking, bitter experience. "How can something so beautiful turn out to be so horrible?" she asked me in anguish. "I have cried so much there are no tears left. I keep telling myself it isn't true, but it is."

Barb was only 16, but a picture of misery. She had come to me for counseling, but the damage had been done. Now she wanted help for the future. She wore a maternity dress and would be having a baby in a month or so. What should have been a "blessed event" for a happily married woman was instead fear and shame because this girl was not married and the father of the baby had run away.

Barb had met Mac about a year before at a basketball game. After the game he offered to buy her a Coke. He told her he was from out of town and worked in a drugstore. He was lonesome because he was new in town.

Her folks did not like it when she came home with a strange boy. He kept telephoning for a date, but they would not let her go out with him. He was too old for her, they said.

Barb begged and complained and pouted, and then rebelliously stopped studying her school assignments. Finally her folks gave in and let her date Mac on weekends.

"Oh, how wonderful to be in love," she sighed deliciously.

They went for walks, hand in hand. Soon it was arm in arm and cheek to cheek. A goodnight kiss turned into passionate kisses.

---

[3] Blanton, Smiley, "How To Handle Temptation," *The Readers Digest* 78:469 (May, 1951) p. 188.

Her parents kept objecting, but they let her continue the weekend dates to keep her happy. A faint guilt lingered over this disagreement with her parents, but she quickly forgot it.

The kissing and petting became unrestrained. And then...it had all seemed so natural, but there were pangs of regret. As guilt flooded her heart, she told him they should not be so intimate with each other. They quarreled about it, and then kissed and made up. When Barb told Mac she was going to have a baby, he exploded in a tantrum. He cursed her stupidity and left her—for good.

"He said he loved me," wailed Barb to me in the counseling room. I did not need to tell her that he was a liar. He loved his pleasure, his freedom—himself. But so did she.

"Why didn't my parents stop me?" Barb sobbed.

But she knew she had fought bitterly with her parents over this. She thought she had found the prince charming of her life. Barb had not yet learned that what is thrilling and pleasant is not always right and good.

Moderation or self-control is not God's invention to make life miserable; it is a law of life for guiding us safely and happily to God's destination. He is near; it makes sense to know Him and please Him, and to ask Him to help you. Barb would tell you that she had no intention of becoming pregnant. She lost control of herself. She learned that it is difficult to control sexual passion that has been stimulated. It all seemed so right to her. Poor Barb felt mistreated and misunderstood by her parents. Mac encouraged her to give them a hard time. They told each other that their friendship was beautiful and wonderful.

They would stand together against these parents who would interfere with young love. The sensations, thrills, and ecstasies of being together were worth fighting for.[4]

Today Barb would tell you to "turn you back on the turbulent desires of youth. Do not give way to your lusts."

Abigail Van Buren, a popular newspaper columnist, has a pithy word for young people:

"Quicker than a penguin sliding down an icicle—that's how quick a necking session can turn into a jam session. And you're the one in the jam!

Troubles are like photographs. They are developed in dark places. Sitting for hours in a dark room or a parked car and kiss-kiss-kissing is ask-ask-asking for trouble. Prolonged kissing is...the first step in serious love-making. It whets the appetite. It is meant to warm up the engines in preparation for a trip to the moon on gossamer wings. And once the engine is warmed up, it's rugged trying to turn it off. 'I couldn't help myself,' is the wail in my mail. But my cry in reply is, 'Who asked you to warm up the engines?' I cannot be

---

[4] This incident appeared originally in *Adult Power*, April 8, 1952, and is used by permission.

more emphatic when I say, 'Keep away from tempting situations!' Avoid 'overparking.' You can get a ticket to some pretty unpleasant places. Double date. Do not invite him over when nobody's home. Stick with the gang on those beach parties. There is safety in numbers. Girls need to 'prove their love' through illicit sex relations like a moose needs a hat rack. Clear the cobwebs out of your head: any fellow who asks you to 'prove your love' is trying to take you for the biggest, most gullible fool who ever walked. That proving bit is one of the oldest and rottenest lines ever invented. Does he love you? It does not sound like it. Someone who loves you wants whatever is best for you...A boy who loves a girl would sooner cut off his right arm than hurt her."[5]

LUST VERSUS LOVE

There's a difference between lust and love. It is easy to confuse the two terms. In magazines and newspapers many of the advertisements use the embracing of two people to catch your eye. Book covers leave little to the imagination. A boy may say, "I had a girl out last night and loved her up." A headline in the paper read, "Two Die Keeping Love Tryst." Movie placards scream "Let's Make Love." One song title, as do many others, plead "Let Me Love You Tonight."

In my teen days the song "That Old Feeling" was popular. It describes love as a heart-stopping thrill when "you" go by. The suggestion is that if the sight of a certain person "thrills" you, it must be love. You are bombarded all day long by music on radio and television with songs that identify love with lust. The emphasis is on "falling" in love. At the same time that young people are becoming aware of a natural attraction toward the opposite sex, they are hit on all sides by the idea that passion and thrill is love. Psychologists call this infatuation. It is a physical attraction based on looks and personality, and is often against their better judgment. It is not based on a state of respect and comradeship that develops when there are similar ideas, tastes, and hopes.

IS SEX AN UNMANAGEABLE URGE?

Attraction between the sexes is not something that occurs between you and one particular person alone. The attraction can be toward many persons—even a stranger. We often hear of the "strong, unmanageable sex urge." This urge is unmanageable only when outside influences fan it. Pictures, stimulating reading material, daydreams, conversations, and physical contact will fan this urge.

Any desire can be fanned. Even the desire for a new car can be fanned to be all-important. You can think about cars, read about them, and watch other people drive them. The desire for a car can cause you to do without other things in order to have one. If you want a car badly enough, you will buy it even if it causes strained relations at home.

---

[5] Reprinted with the permission of Bernard Geis Associates from "Dear Teenager" by Abigail Van Buren. Copyrighted 1959 by Phillips-Van Buren Inc. And Bernard Geis Associates, joint venture.

The sex urge can be fanned in the same way. You can talk about the opposite sex, read about, and look at pictures of sex. You can constantly watch for things that excite you. This is a deliberate effort at keeping the sex urge fanned.

Popenoe gives six reasons why young people are stimulated to experiment with sex:

1. Curiosity.
2. Desire to feel "grown up."
3. Desire for "adventure."
4. Gang spirit; afraid of being thought a sissy.
5. Anxiety about being abnormal and desire to reassure oneself.
6. Virtual seduction by an older person.[7]

He adds that authorities who have studied the problems of prostitution declare that boys who frequent houses of ill fame are not driven by an unmanageable urge. Rather, for the most part they are fearful, uneasy, embarrassed, and ashamed. Seldom does a teenager enter such a place alone. Usually two boys or more go together, egged on by one another.

Most boys sooner or later, will be faced with the temptation to visit such a place. An assortment of underworld characters make a living by encouraging young people to patronize their business.

The Bible gives an account of a young man being contacted by a prostitute:

With her enticing speech she caused him to yield, With her flattering lips she seduced him. Immediately he went after her, as an ox goes to the slaughter, Or as a fool to the correction of the stocks, Till an arrow struck his liver. As a bird hastens to the snare, He did not know it would take his life. Now therefore, listen to me, my children; Pay attention to the words of my mouth: Do not let your heart turn aside to her ways, Do not stray into her paths; For she has cast down many wounded, And all who were slain by her were strong men. Her house is the way to hell, Descending to the chambers of death.
PROVERBS 7:21-27

Every boy should be armed against the easy-going or loose girl. Dickerson warns that "...the boy should know also that the easy-going girl who is by no means a prostitute may likewise be a source of venereal disease. Any girl who permits one boy to be intimate with her is likely to permit others. And there is no assurance that some of these others may not have gonorrhea or syphilis and leave germs behind

---

[7] Popenoe, Paul, *Building Sex Into Your Life,* The American Institute of Family Relations, Los Angeles, 1944.

them to be transferred to any boy who comes after them. The loose girl may be a carrier just as the prostitute may be."[8]

The aggressive boy can be just as dangerous. The girl who has been involved sexually with only her steady may become infected. In his book, *None of These Diseases*, Dr. S. L. McMillen discusses such a case.

> A girl who had sexual relations with only one boyfriend thought she was safe. She was terribly shocked when her doctor told her she was infected. A 'venereal tracer' revealed: the boy had consorted with only one other girl. This girl had had relations with five other men, who in turn had been with nineteen women, some of them prostitutes. The girl who thought her relationship had been limited to one person had had contact, through him, with at least ninety-two others."[9]

Even more subtle and harmful than organized vice is the parade of paperbacks available at the corner drugstore. For years fictional works have portrayed sexual looseness. Now, however, non-fiction works are recommending premarital relations as a way of life. Books deal with sex and the single girl, sex on the campus, sex and the career girl, and sex and the office girl. These are impassioned arguments for sex outside of marriage.

WHY PARENTS ARE CONCERNED

The freedom that young people have today adds to the conflict. The automobile presents parents and teens with a grave problem. It allows two people to sit together very closely. Parents know the strong attraction that closeness brings with it. Teens feel confident of their ability to handle these close relationships.

"Don't you trust me?" is the heated retort that many a young person has hurled at parents. The answer should be, "No." You should not even trust yourself. It is a fact of life that physical closeness is sexually stimulating and hard to manage.

Dr. Dickerson, an experienced health educator, offers four guidelines to parents. See what you think of them:[10]

> 1. Do not permit the young adolescent the opportunity to pet. Boys and girls at 13 and 14 want to be by themselves. They may resent observation of parents. Dickerson says it is foolish to rely too much on immature judgment and self-control. It is only fair and smart to have older people around.

---

[8] Dickerson, Roy E., Home Study Course, American Institute of Family Relations, Los Angeles, 1947, pp. 55, 56.

[9] McMillen, Dr. S. I., *None of These Diseases*, Fleming H. Revell Company, West Wald, New Jersey, 1959, p. 43.

[10] Dickerson, op. Cit., pp. 51, 52.

2. Point out that there is always danger in trifling with sexual desire. The only sure plan is to avoid sexual stimulation. You can separate, change the subject, get out of a dark corner, and join the crowd.

3. Cultivate in youth the feeling that any intimacy without affection is distasteful. We enjoy intimacy with those we love and shrink from it otherwise—in spite of the physical thrill. There is something tawdry and out of place, a cheap substitute when you are intimate with a casual acquaintance.

4. Where there is a religious background in the home, these intimacies should be discussed with the child against that background.

There they are. These are the responsibilities that parents need to face. Teens usually take a rather dim view of such parental supervision. They feel quite capable of handling themselves in dating situations. The facts and records of distraught teens and unwed mothers prove that parents have a reason for concern. They must trust you as a person. They realize however that strong desire can easily get out of hand. The fact is that adults as well as teens can easily lose control of emotions when they are aroused.

Parents can understand that their children tend to chafe under their watchful eye. Teens can understand that their parents' interest and close supervision is intended to help them manage a powerful urge.

WHAT ABOUT KISSING GOOD NIGHT?

A difficult question. Perhaps the answer lies in the reason for the kiss. Does it mean, "Good night, my friend, it's been real"? Or is it an invitation for more? The girl must be the judge. A short good-night kiss, not intended to arouse the passions of either of you seems acceptable. Kissing does arouse passion, and high school dating is hardly the reason for doing so. When a short kiss leads to two, it is no longer saying "Good night and thank you." It is saying, "Let's not go yet, let's become aroused."

You must be the judge. You are the steward of your own body. It will take a higher goal to carry you through. It takes a power not your own. There is help if you want it. The help comes from God. The Apostle points the way:

> God's plan is to make you holy, and that entails first of all a clean cut with sexual immorality. Everyone of you should learn to control his body, keeping it pure and treating it with respect, and never regarding it as an instrument for self-gratification, as do pagans with no knowledge of God. You cannot break this rule without in some way cheating your fellow men. And you must remember that God will punish all who do offend in this matter, and we have warned you how we have seen this work out in our experience of life. The calling of God is not to impurity but to

the most thorough purity, and anyone who makes light of the matter is not making light of a man's ruling but of God's command. It is not for nothing that the Spirit of God given us is called the Holy Spirit."

1 THESSALONIANS 4:3-8 (PHILLIPS)

The sex urge can be managed. You can be careful what you look at, what you read, what you are willing to listen to, and what you are willing to do. God will help you if you want His help.

The Bible says,

If you believe in goodness and if you value the approval of God, fix your minds on the things which are holy and right and pure and beautiful and good.

PHILIPPIANS 4:8 (PHILLIPS)

There are two sides to the coin. What the Bible says makes sense. You know it is right, but the temptation to enjoy the pleasure of sexual thinking and sexual contact is strong. You enjoy the freedom of making your own choice.

Outside of marriage, sex relations bring guilt, shame, loss of respect, fear of discovery, hiding, and even lying to cover up. In short, it spoils the relationship.

One girl had premarital relations with her boyfriend and broke up with him. She met another man whom she greatly respected. What should she do? Tell him? She did not want to be a cheat and she was afraid gossip would get to him.

Another girl became involved with a boy. She was sure he loved her and that they would eventually legalize their relationship. After some time he revealed a side of his character she had never known. He could not resist the temptation to talk to the boys about his affairs! After breaking off this relationship, the girl found it difficult to throw off the reputation of being a loose girl.

One couple was having relations and planning to marry. He was killed in an accident a week before the wedding. In another instance, the fellow was drafted. Separated by miles, they both became suspicious and distrustful.

As you can see, many do not have a good foundation for marriage. Physical temptation is the only common denominator for many who date. But just what is the basis for a good marriage?

THE FOUNDATION FOR A HAPPY MARRIAGE: THE LOVE OF GOD

What is it that binds two people together in marriage? Quite likely you will answer, "Love, of course." "Tell me you love only me," lovers whisper to each other. They are referring to a special kind of feeling, shared completely and exclusively by the marriage partners and kept alive because of each other.

Certainly the Bible teaches that husband and wife should love each other (Titus 2:4; Colossians 3:19). But our Lord also said:

**"You shall love the Lord your God with all your heart,
and with all your soul, and with all your mind."**
MATTHEW 22:37, 38

If you give your undivided love to God, how can you give undivided love to your mate? It would appear at first glance that to love God in the way scripture demands would be to relegate everyone else to second place.

But that isn't all. In writing to the Thessalonians, Paul makes a further demand on your love. He says:

**And may the Lord make you increase and abound in love to
one another and to all, just as we do to you.**
1 THESSALONIANS 3:12

Does this not compound the quandary? How can you love God, your mate, and all men and women? Or does the Bible catalog love as Brand A, Brand B, and Brand C? Is the love you have for your girl-friend different from your love for your mother?

Something that Henry Drummond wrote in the last century may help parents and teens to see how we are to love. In his essay, "The Greatest Thing in the World," he referred to love as described by Paul in 1 Corinthians 13 and likened it to light. If you pass light through a crystal prism, he pointed out, it emerges on the other side of the prism broken into its component parts—red, blue, yellow, violet, orange, and all the colors of the rainbow. In just such a way Paul passes love through the magnificent prism of his inspired intellect and it emerges broken into its basic elements. Drummond calls this the "spectrum of love." It has nine components:

Patience	Love suffereth long
Kindness	and is kind,
Generosity	love envieth not,
Humility	love vaunteth not itself, is not puffed up,
Courtesy	doth not behave itself unseemly,
Unselfishness	seeketh not her own
Good temper	is not easily provoked,
Guilelessness	thinketh no evil,
Sincerity	rejoiceth not in iniquity, but rejoiceth in the truth.

If teens will compare their love for a special friend with this "spectrum of love" they will be able to gauge its genuineness. Study of this list will lead you to understand that as you demonstrate your love for God you will be loving your friends, your family, and your spouse—and, indeed, all men—in the very same love. You will not be loving God in one way, your friend in another way, and others in a third way. In other words, all genuine love comes from God. It is not physical love. It is not ignited and fanned by a person.

Paul leaves no doubt about the source of such love. "The Lord make you to increase, and abound in love one toward another..." The apostle John adds:

> **Beloved, let us love one another, for love is of God;**
> **and everyone who loves is born of God and knows God.**
> 1 JOHN 4:7

Love is a spiritual fruit which comes from God. It can be universally applied. It is to know no limits. Is there anyone in your life to whom you should not be kind, patient, good tempered, sincere, generous, unselfish, and courteous? Is there any occasion where you are justified in being proud or in thinking evil? Love is broader than the union of two people in a marriage. It encompasses this relationship and many others. Thus, it cannot be love that sets one man and woman apart as the twain that shall become one flesh.

If love does not make marriage unique, what is it? It is the exclusive and *unique relationship*—the duties and details of marriage—that sets a man and a woman apart.

Teens need to realize that the relationship of marriage is no guarantor of love. A husband and wife may live under the same roof, spend each other's money, sleep in the same room, eat together, give birth to children from a shared physical experience, and still not demonstrate genuine love as revealed in 1 Corinthians 13. Can they be said to love each other when they lack patience, kindness, courteousness, unselfishness and the other qualities that make up genuine love? No. Without the undergirding of the love that comes from God, the intimacies of the marriage relationship can drive a couple apart. The dating relationship will also suffer if it is not motivated by the love of God.

The teen who yields himself to the love of God produces a perfect love toward others, including his dating partner. He can trust his judgment when it comes to finding his marriage partner and can start life together with a clear conscience.

Again we turn to the Bible to learn the true nature of love. There we read:

> **This love of which I speak is slow to lose patience—it looks for a way of being constructive. It is not possessive; it is neither anxious to impress nor does it cherish inflated ideas of its own importance. Love has good manners and does not pursue selfish advantage. It is not touchy. It does not keep account of evil or gloat over the wickedness of other people. On the contrary, it is glad with all good men when truth prevails. Love knows no limit to its endurance, no end to its trust, no fading of its hope; it can outlast anything. It is, in fact, the one thing that still stands when all else has fallen.**
> 1 CORINTHIANS 13:4-8 (PHILLIPS)

For love is as strong as death, Jealousy as cruel as the grave; Its flames are flames of fire, A most vehement flame. Many waters cannot quench love, Nor can the floods drown it. If a man would give for love All the wealth of his house, It would be utterly despised.

SONG OF SOLOMON 8:6, 7